SUCCESSFUL CENTERS

Standards-Based Learning Centers that Work

Author
Lisa B. Fiore, Ph.D.

SHELL EDUCATION

Consultant

Tiffany Fadin, M.A.Ed.
Teacher and Reading Specialist

Publishing Credits

Robin Erickson, *Production Director;* Lee Aucoin, *Creative Director;*
Timothy J. Bradley, *Illustration Manager;* Sara Johnson, M.S.Ed., *Editorial Director;*
Jennifer Viñas, *Editor;* Grace Alba, *Designer;* Corinne Burton, M.A.Ed., *Publisher*

Image Credits

all images Shutterstock

Shell Education

5301 Oceanus Drive
Huntington Beach, CA 92649-1030
http://www.shelleducation.com
ISBN 978-1-4258-1019-1
© 2014 Shell Education Publishing, Inc.

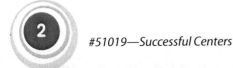

Table of Contents

A major reason that we have not become extinct is that we play…we are good at lots of things rather than expert at just a few.

—Bob Hughes (2012)

Success at the Center

In recent years, teaching professionals have found themselves to be working in an exciting yet challenging climate for teachers of young children—when "success" is often measured in test scores, and children and teachers find themselves in a competitive climate, "racing to the top." It is not always easy to focus on what is developmentally appropriate for young children when pressures for children to learn academic skills contradict over 100 years of research about how children learn. Early childhood educators inherently know what matters most to children in the classroom, and it can be summed up as a love of learning and strong, trusting relationships (Fiore 2012). These powerful relationships exist as mutual, bidirectional relationships between teachers, children, and components of the classroom environment, and extend to families and the broader community. Early childhood educators also know that keeping these values at the center of early childhood educational experiences is the best way to ensure success for all learners.

So what exactly *are* learning centers? For the purposes of this book, learning centers are both physical and intellectual spaces. In terms of physical spaces, learning centers are indeed small areas in a classroom that are designated for specific, focused learning. For example, a carpeted area in the classroom might be the permanent Block Center, deemed so primarily because the carpeting helps to ensure that the block play noise is muffled to some extent. In terms of intellectual spaces, learning centers have no bounds—they are limited only by the creativity that teachers and children bring into the classroom on a daily basis. In other words, learning centers are significant because they relate to children's interests, motivation, and stages of development. Learning centers complement concepts and activities that children have experienced in other classroom lessons, yet they allow children to be the driving forces behind the depth and extension of the learning experiences. For example, the birth of a new sibling for one child might launch a hospital center that can bridge science, literacy, math, art, and music curricula. The centers invite children to engage with appropriate materials and enable them to explore and work independently or with partners or small groups as active learners.

This book focuses on learning centers, not simply as distinct areas of a classroom, but representative of a fundamental approach to teaching and learning that places children at the core. It recognizes the important and complex roles of the teacher: as guide, co-learner, and key source of support. The first sections of this book define learning centers, and describe the importance of them in the context of children's development—cognitive, social, and physical. Keeping success at the center of planning does not require prescribed, teacher-directed activities with predetermined outcomes. This book provides 70 activities that capitalize on the wisdom of teachers. Furthermore, these activities help nurture a teacher disposition that welcomes a balance between decision making and possibilities as well as the challenges associated with incorporating effective learning center experiences.

Introduction and Research *(cont.)*

For teachers, striking a balance in early childhood classrooms involves keeping an eye toward the future, knowing children's developmental pathways and what they will be expected to achieve in subsequent years, and staying grounded in the moment, noticing where children are as individuals and members of the larger group. The adoption of the Common Core State Standards in virtually all of the American states has prompted educators to form new and different associations with the term "the core" (Gewertz 2012), when early childhood educators instinctively associate "core" with "heart," "central," or "most important." It is one thing to know about child development but quite another to provide children with classroom activities that promote problem solving, interpersonal skill development and practice, and responsibility.

Some of the big questions addressed in this book are:

- How can centers be used to nurture children's emerging interests and also meet required standards?

- How can teachers mine the "mess" and articulate the skills that develop out of everyday experiences?

- How can teachers best communicate with families about the merits of play-based activities?

Learning centers provide opportunities for teachers to work with children in authentic, meaningful ways, keeping children hands-on and engaged at the center. The activities in this book are the result of much collaboration, conversation, and observation. Learning centers complement curriculum for early childhood teachers who consider children to be active, curious, and competent and know that "joy and learning are not at opposite ends of the teaching spectrum" (Fiore 2012, xii). In many cases the learning centers *become* the curriculum in a supportive environment.

This book translates important theoretical and philosophical foundations of early childhood education through concrete center activities across a range of content areas. For example, all child development courses emphasize theories about the ways children actively construct learning and the value of social interactions with peers and others. Building upon theories and approaches to documenting young children, such as the Reggio Emilia approach to early childhood education, teachers can examine measures of accountability and strengthen their understanding of mindful, flexible, and creative teaching—recognizing the power of ordinary, sometimes messy moments of learning and extending the experiences for children, families, and others in the community.

Creating a Classroom Culture

Whether we use the word *curious, inquisitive, flexible,* or *supportive,* there is no doubt that early childhood educators recognize the qualities of a strong teacher. These same qualities can be used to describe young children and can be nurtured in effective classroom environments that highlight the importance of letting children follow their instincts, test their own hypotheses, and experience learning on their own terms. As mentioned previously, many teachers experience a tension in their classroom setting that hinders such effective activity—tension between the powerful pressure of accountability and the desire to allow children freedom to explore and time to follow their ideas. Indeed, teachers are responsible for guiding children's thinking so that they are able to reach new milestones and levels of understanding. Teachers are also responsible for guiding and sustaining a healthy and productive classroom culture. When milestones and guidelines for experiences become more like benchmarks that must be met, teachers, administrators, and families grow increasingly concerned about children "making the grade" at earlier ages.

A classroom culture that incorporates learning centers is more than simply arranging furniture in separate parts of the room so that curriculum may be taught at distinct tables. Setting goals and measuring outcomes are intrinsically woven into the fabric of the environment, and the activities and materials at each center must be thoughtfully selected so that every member of the class is exposed to developmentally appropriate, culturally sensitive experiences:

> The climate is one in which "learning is cool," worth engaging in, and everyone— teacher and students—is involved in the process of learning. It is a climate in which it is okay to acknowledge that the process of learning is rarely linear, requires commitment and investment of effort, and has many ups and downs in knowing, not knowing, and in building confidence that we *can* know. It is a climate in which error is welcomed, in which student questioning is high, in which engagement is the norm, and in which students gain reputations as effective learners (Hattie 2012, 26).

It is important to note that a classroom culture that incorporates learning centers does not run counter to legislative mandates. District, state, and/or federal curriculum objectives can certainly guide activities that early childhood learners experience. Specific tasks that are featured at distinct centers should include tasks that lend themselves to the development of skills and understandings deemed appropriate for a grade level. The systematic use of learning centers helps teachers and children bring learning goals together in developmentally appropriate ways.

Early childhood classrooms often include a variety of learning centers. Teachers can strike a balance between permanent centers such as art and math and thematic centers that grow out of children's specific interests and therefore change over time. This book integrates learning across curricula in that permanent centers may anchor some desired learning outcomes yet provide opportunities for children to strengthen skills through activities that are not limited to one exclusive domain. For example, the math center may include a computer that children use to type math news stories. Thus, children are gaining literacy skills while focusing on math concepts. The classroom culture supports clear expectations for learning center activities, but the centers are not simply areas for children to complete closed-ended exercises. Research has shown that "the best and most productive centers involve open-ended inquiry" (Fountas and Pinnell 1996, 49).

The open-ended quality of learning center experiences contained in this book relieves teachers of the pressure to develop new lessons and activities every day. The classroom culture shapes the use of the learning centers and supports routines that children come to master. Young children learn how to access and explore the materials, and teachers are therefore able to focus their attention in numerous ways. The centers listed below are highlighted in this book but are not intended to represent a definitive list of possible learning centers. Some features of each center are included here, and will be discussed in greater detail in the sections that follow.

Center Type	This center supports understanding and development of:	
Math	• attributes of objects • patterns • seriation • classification	• matching • concept of number • sequence • math vocabulary
Language and Literacy	• concepts of print • concepts of writing • foundations for reading • books and publishing • poetry • language and vocabulary development	• storytelling • plot/sequence • characters • mastery with writing tools and paper

Center Type	This center supports understanding and development of:	
Science	• science concepts • connections with nature • problem solving • scientific thinking	• delay of gratification • cause and effect • living vs. nonliving things
Social Studies	• appreciation of diversity • time, chronology, and sequence • maps and geography	• citizenship and responsibility
Art	• fine-motor skills • art concepts	• self-expression • creative expression
Music	• appreciation of different styles of music • singing • music concepts	• rhythm and rhyme • aural discrimination
Mystery	• mindfulness • resilience • empathy	• self-regulation • personal strengths • creativity

Fortunately, most early childhood classrooms are designed in a manner that supports the use of learning centers. Most early childhood classrooms do not feature rows or clusters of desks where children are expected to sit for extended periods of time while the teacher stands at the front of the room imparting jewels of wisdom. Sadly, as pressures relating to accountability for teachers and schools have increased, many Pre-K and kindergarten classrooms have become "…devoid of materials, eerily silent, where children sit as teachers drill them on facts from a prescribed curriculum. Classrooms where teachers spend long hours testing individual children at a computer while the rest of the class sit copying from the board—no talking" (Carlsson-Paige 2012).

The following examples provide two different classroom layouts for your consideration. While you will note the placement of specific learning centers, it is perfectly acceptable, and even desirable, to move the location of specific centers throughout the year. As you introduce specific centers to children, a flexible approach to the classroom design will serve you and the children well. It has also been shown that supportive classroom environments directly impact the brain through production of serotonin and dopamine, which "play a crucial part in how students feel and learn" (Biller 2003, 25).

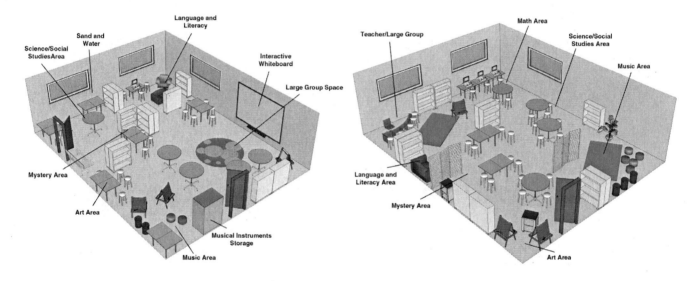

Over the course of a school year, as you develop a richer understanding of the members of the classroom, learning centers will provide countless opportunities for children to learn with and from their peers in a nonjudgmental way. In the section that follows, we will consider the relationship between learning centers and the major players in early childhood classrooms.

Players and Protagonists

Seasoned early childhood teachers are used to questions from parents and caregivers that sound something like this: "When are children going to do some real learning?"

Of course these questions often come on the heels of numerous exchanges between adults and children that sound something like this:

Adult: "What did you do at school today?"

Child: "Nothing. We just played."

The discomfort or unease that caregivers feel when they are worried that playing means "not learning" is similar to the discomfort that teachers may initially feel when they hear that learning centers are based in play and that children are therefore the primary players. The Reggio Emilia approach to early childhood education (inspired by the work of early childhood educators in Reggio Emilia, Italy), considered by a growing number of educators around the world to be "the gold standard for quality early childhood education" (New 2007, 1), and at the core of the best schools in the world for young children (Kantrowitz and Wingert 1991), is anchored in several key concepts. One of those concepts is that children are "protagonists" in their own growth and learning. That is, they are powerful and capable and are active constructors of their own learning (Edwards, Gandini, and Forman 2011). Seen in this light, children's play takes on a different meaning—it is not that children learn in spite of play, but that they learn *through* play. Play is important for children's development of symbolic thinking, self-regulation, and empathy as well as skills in math and literacy and is the thread that is woven throughout the center-based activities in this book.

When families are acknowledged as partners in their children's education, they are often more receptive to teachers' decisions about curriculum and understand teachers' respect for play as a fundamental resource of childhood. Researchers have underscored the need for play in children's development, citing it as "the delicate dance of childhood that strengthens the mind and body, and nourishes the soul" (Frost 2010, xviii), recognized throughout human evolution as "a deep and irresistible urge to explore, experiment with, and have knowledge of the world, the universe, and everything" (Hughes 2012, 80).

Thoughtful design and implementation of classroom center experiences paired with thoughtful assessment and communication with families can bridge the gap between mandated goals set for young children and developmentally appropriate practices. For example, educators of young children recognize that play is a core resource of childhood (Carlsson-Paige 2009; Meier, Engel, and Taylor 2010), and that play is sometimes messy. While some people are uncomfortable with mess and consider play to be merely frivolous, advocates for young children possess an attitude that supports play in all of its forms as crucial to development (Henig 2008).

Attitude

As we consider engaging children in center activities, it is also important to recognize the role of adult support in the design of learning center activities for young children and the impact of teachers' attitudes on children's learning experiences and developing self-concepts. For example, some teachers worry that the noise level in their classrooms will be too high if children are at learning centers. Clearly, every teacher has a different personal level of tolerance for noise and activity. Rather than dismiss learning centers as too noisy or potentially disruptive, teachers can employ simple strategies to help reduce the classroom noise level, such as limiting the number of students working together at each center. The social benefits that children gain from learning to take turns, negotiating for resources, and taking another's perspective are reflected in their enjoyment and engagement. Teachers may find that there are strategic reasons for pairing students rather than grouping them in threes and fours. "When there are just two students, each has to do a bigger share of the work and the thinking" (Diller 2011, 9). Children remain actively involved in their own learning, and the positive experiences reinforce their engagement, which has been shown to lead to longer attention spans and greater retention of material (Prince 2004, 93).

Early childhood teachers who are required to cover specific mandated curricula can structure activities at specific learning centers (e.g., math, literacy, art, music, science) that complement classroom curricula. The flexibility afforded by the use of learning centers provides natural opportunities for extending and enhancing classroom learning, while honoring children's individual learning styles, interests, and abilities. A respect for children's individual needs is matched by teachers' decisions about specific activities at the learning centers. However, it is important to note the following:

> "A pedagogy of fairness is not to be confused with more familiar goals in early childhood education, such as sharing and cooperation. These are important civic standards of classroom life, of course, but they are outcomes of fair teaching, not one and the same. Fair teaching encompasses all that honors young children's need to be sought out and valued, to be remembered, by the teacher and the group regardless of their race, gender, popularity, or developmental difference (Cooper 2011, 94)."

Above all else, children's thinking must be challenged and their hearts and minds must be stimulated. Since most classrooms accommodate children from varied backgrounds and developmental levels, understanding children in the class helps determine the variety of learning centers, activities, and materials that are most appropriate year to year for each unique group.

One of the most common concerns for early childhood teachers is how to support English language learners in the classroom. Effective early childhood teachers possess a strong desire to respect and nurture children's native languages while simultaneously helping children develop strong English skills. Most teachers of young children receive little to no explicit instruction in skills and strategies to help children who are English language learners, yet a supportive attitude goes a long way in helping children navigate classroom curriculum. Page 199 features ways that learning centers may contribute to success for children who are English language learners—in the classroom as well as in their own beliefs about themselves as capable learners.

At a basic level, learning centers promote cooperation among children who may choose oral and/or written language to express their ideas, solve problems, and communicate with peers. Learning center experiences provide authentic opportunities for children that standardized curriculum may not provide, such as building associations between objects and new vocabulary words and taking risks when speaking with peers. By providing real items and natural materials, teachers promote children's mastery over concepts and encourage participation. Teachers' beliefs in and commitments to students have tremendous effects on children's achievement. Young children are most eager to demonstrate their competence when presented with thoughtfully designed learning challenges.

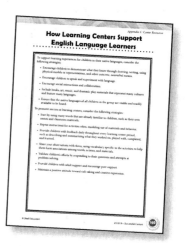

Managing Learning Centers

The word *managing* is a bit misleading, because it may evoke an assumption that the teacher is the sole manager. Effective early childhood teachers know that children should not be expected to take sole responsibility for their learning center experiences. Teachers must always provide quality instruction, and they connect this work with increasing opportunities for independent practice among small groups of children. Over time, however, children and teachers become co-managers of the learning centers. In a supportive classroom climate, the desire to maintain engaging learning centers is shared among all class members, and the investment in choice of activities and themes is strong, almost second nature. For a list of suggestions for gradually incorporating learning centers into the classroom, see pages 200–201.

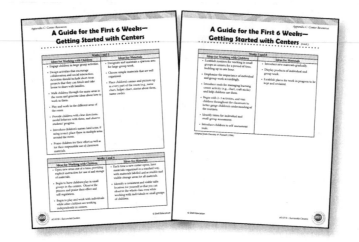

Young children experience very few instances when they are in control of their choices. Throughout the course of a given day, teachers and caregivers choose for children what time to wake up, which clothes to wear, which foods to eat (or avoid), what activities to engage in, and when to rest. Developmental theorists recognize the struggles that naturally occur between the growing child and caregivers as children's cognitive and physical development enables them to accomplish more tasks. Learning centers provide children opportunities to exercise informed decision making and to realize the consequences of their actions and inaction, as the case may be. Whether children choose the music center or the science center, the very act of making a selection allows them to see themselves as children who are in charge. Making choices at learning centers helps young children feel powerful and is a fundamental feature of a democratic society. Like freedom, imagination has no limits.

Why is this important? One reason is that when children feel a part of a group in which they are free to exercise their opinions and their choices are respected and supported, then the buy-in helps support the use of learning centers. The fact that children are expected to make their own decisions conveys to them that the teacher trusts their choices. This, in turn, serves to extend and reinforce curriculum and contributes to students' success. Research indicates that children who demonstrate an ability to plan and monitor their own behavior experience greater success in school. This self-regulation is evident in children's use of time and mastery or task completion.

Use of Time

The amount of time that early childhood teachers allocate for learning center activities varies depending on the school, the teacher, the agenda, and the children. At the beginning of the year, teachers may involve the children in primarily large-group activities, and over time, the amount of time shifts to include more independent learning center time. While children are gaining a better sense of classroom routines, a relatively short center time of approximately 10–15 minutes is important. The goal is to promote their sense of independence and familiarity with materials. A successful learning center time may be as simple as going to a center, engaging in an activity, and cleaning up when time is up. Once all learning centers have been introduced, center time may be adjusted to coincide with children's attention spans and the number of activities offered. When children are totally engaged in an activity, they are more likely to experience the completely focused, joyful learning that has been referred to as "flow" (Csikszentmihalyi 2008). Ideally, learning center times should reach 45 minutes to one hour in order for children to enjoy maximum involvement in play and to be free from pressures to hurry their choices.

What *does* time mean to a young child, really? For many children, time can be measured in units that relate to their personal lives and experiences, such as the period between breakfast and snack time or the length of a favorite cartoon episode. To expect all children to regulate themselves according to a clock is not realistic, although some children may be able to tell time at a very young age, especially if using a digital clock. Teachers of young children try to develop strategies to help children pace themselves during a learning center time, such as five-minute warnings, a soft bell or other tone, and colored cards placed on the tables when it is time to finish up and move on. These types of simple techniques help children with their own pacing and mastery over the routine.

Mastery and Task Completion

For young children, habits of engagement are linked to their use of time. When children remain at a particular center, they are practicing their ability to focus on tasks and to collaborate with peers. They repeat some activities and learn to take reasonable risks as they attempt new activities. As children gain mastery over content through repetition of tasks and exposure to different tasks, they are better able to link specific skills to the application of the skill in their daily lives. Skills that are introduced in one center can be reinforced in a different center and in a thematic unit. Integrating aspects of various disciplines provides children with meaningful work, rather than boring, disconnected tasks to complete.

As noted previously, it is important for all children to experience a balance of activities. Formal and informal learning experiences should be used because some children learn better in structured activities. The greater the variety of centers, the more opportunity children have to exercise their preferences and develop self-awareness.

When children's learning styles and strengths are exercised, they are able to make connections between theory and application. Working in small groups encourages healthy tensions that lead to new and richer understandings and natural opportunities for differentiated instruction. For tools to help children and teachers plan and monitor children's use of various learning centers, see pages 202–203. At times, some children will prefer work in a parallel style, exploring materials and activities independently. Other times, such as when playing games with one to two peers, students will support and scaffold one another along the path to reaching their mutual goals. One result of children's successful completion of assigned tasks, which cannot be minimized, is that children view themselves as successful learners. Young children and teachers become partners in the learning process, with shared expectations and responsibilities for learning center content and customs.

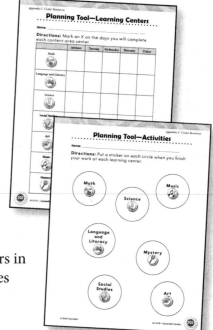

Assessment

In a climate that reduces much of children's learning processes to measurable outcomes, the use of learning centers opens possibilities for teachers (and students) to support the needs of every member of the classroom. Instead of assessment being an added burden, teachers can use strategies for facilitating learning center use as methods of formative and summative evaluation. For example, the learning center assessment charts (pages 205–207) can be used to record children's progress through the various centers over the course of a week or several weeks. Teachers can note how long children spend at a particular learning center, whether children complete their tasks (successfully or unsuccessfully), which centers appeal to different children over time, which children tend to gravitate toward each other, and where conflict frequently lies. As a result of informal assessment, teachers can note how simple adjustments to the classroom environment can have a big impact on children's learning.

Taking a step back to assess the big picture, such as the classroom layout, is one simple way to assess how learning centers are being used and the value that they add to the classroom. To gain a sense of this big picture, see page 204.

By shifting from assessment of the environment to that of the individual child and small groups of children, valuable information can be gathered through simple observations. The sections that follow will provide suggested use of the activities and deeper discussion about watching, listening, and documentating as methods of assessing students' processes and products. A key component of successful assessment is exhibited in the attitude of the teacher and is demonstrated through thoughtful reflection before, during, and after activities are introduced at learning centers.

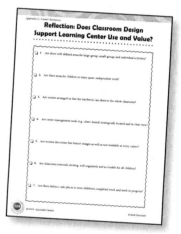

Looking, Listening, and Learning

The key is curiosity, and it is curiosity, not answers that we model. As we seek to know more about a child, we demonstrate the acts of observing, listening, questioning, and wondering. When we are curious about a child's words and our responses to those words, the child feels respected. The child is respected. What are the ideas that I have that are so interesting to the teacher? I must be somebody with good ideas.

—Vivian Paley (1986)

The practice of using learning centers with young children is more than a "set it up and let 'em go" approach to learning. Early childhood educators are actively involved in the processes, tools, and benefits associated with the systematic use of classroom learning centers. Teachers make daily decisions that impact classroom environment, rules, and expectations for children's development. Paying close attention to children, using a variety of methods, makes it less likely that we will see what we want to see and miss (or ignore) what we do not want to see. Looking at learning center activities and listening closely to the players help teachers better understand young children's learning.

Documentation

Documentation means more than checklists, more than photographs, and more than pretty bulletin board displays. Documentation "is not just a teaching tool" but a way of "knowing and valuing children" (Turner & Wilson 2010, 5).

What separates documentation from ordinary assessment of children's learning is its relationship to process and products. In many cases, assessment is focused on an end goal or product without valuing the process. Early childhood researchers who routinely document children's and teachers' learning often compare the process to that of detectives or anthropologists. Teachers may use different techniques to observe and document children's learning, but the attitude they possess is similar. What they share is an underlying desire to learn something that will benefit the classroom culture and strengthen their teaching.

Italian educator Carlina Rinaldi (2001) has described the role of documentation in teaching and learning:

> At the moment of documentation (observation and interpretation), the element of assessment enters the picture immediately, that is, in the context and during the time in which the experience (activity) takes place. It is not sufficient to make an abstract prediction that establishes what is significant—the elements of value necessary for learning to be achieved—before the documentation is actually carried out. It is necessary to interact with the action itself, with that which is revealed, defined, and perceived as truly significant, as the experience unfolds (85).

Looking, Listening, and Learning (cont.)

Documentation positions teachers as co-learners in the classroom through a thoughtful process of recording, analyzing, and sharing observations of young children. During learning center periods, teachers and children engage in activities that are documented in photos, video clips, and samples of children's work and conversation. This, in turn, has the potential to inspire further exploration.

When teachers try to capture a full, accurate essence of a child, they realize that it is impossible to record every single detail of any center activity. "Whether it is because a teacher is looking down at her paper while jotting down notes, or because a video camera is angled a certain way and therefore misses one corner of the classroom, it is crucial to note that no one observation is perfect" (Fiore 2011, 47). It is also true that no one observation can be expected to represent a child's full range of abilities. Several factors contribute to successful observation and documentation. All children and teachers are known to have "off" days, so any documentation process must include several opportunities to observe every child, using different tools to gather information.

A solid strategy for observing during learning center periods is useful for many reasons and prompts teachers to ask themselves questions such as:

- *What is a realistic amount of time that I will be able to observe children at learning centers each day?*

- *How can I prepare the classroom so that I may observe while children are engaged in activity?*

- *How will I reflect on and share my documentation?*

- *With whom will I share my thoughts and seek another perspective?*

- *What are the best methods for documenting young children's learning?*

- *How will I know if children's needs are being met?*

Different approaches to observing children and documenting learning require different amounts of time and materials. The more time needed, the more teachers must rely on a co-teacher or assistant to help with classroom activities while he or she observes.

A note of caution relating to various forms of written notes: These notes are taken as the events are filtered through the lens of one individual. While a teacher is busy writing, he or she may miss some action that therefore does not get included in the notes. Also, because teachers are human, we are all prone to biases based on our own life experiences. It sometimes happens that our notes reflect some of these biases. A useful strategy to minimize the presence and impact of bias is observing with a colleague from time to time. Two sets of eyes often notice different things, and the result of comparing two sets of notes means that teachers will discuss and negotiate interpretations in order to report the most accurate account of events.

Looking, Listening, and Learning *(cont.)*

Active Listening

One factor that contributes to successful observation is the understanding that it is a process that involves many different senses. A teacher most often records information using looking *and* listening. Carlina Rinaldi has written extensively about what she calls "the pedagogy of listening" (Rinaldi 2006, 65). Rinaldi defines listening with an eye (and ear) for detail, weaving the art and practice of listening into practical applications for teachers. When teachers and children use active listening, the teaching and learning relationship changes and children are empowered. The classroom changes from one in which the teacher notices the learning that takes place to one in which learning is created *and* noticed by all members of the group, thereby raising levels of understanding as a result (Fiore and Rosenquest 2010).

Technology

If a teacher chooses to use technology such as an audio recorder or video recorder, these tools can be set up in the classroom—on a table or on a tripod in a corner—and left to record while the teacher goes about the daily routine. At the end of the day, or even a few days later, the teacher can listen to or watch the recordings and see what he or she was unable to see during the moment-to-moment learning center activity. One huge benefit of recording children's learning center activities is that digital audio and video allow teachers unlimited opportunities to revisit interesting moments by simply rewinding and playing again and again.

Not all technology requires electricity or batteries, however. At one time, a mechanical pencil was considered high-tech compared to a standard #2 Ticonderoga. Since all teachers agree that observation entails watching children and usually taking notes, the pace of many classroom settings has made the use of sticky notes a successful practice. Teachers keep pads in their pockets and scribble notes on the papers throughout the day. Teachers then stick those small papers into children's folders to be revisited later. While this system does provide useful information about learning center activity and engagement, such sporadic note taking does not capture or present a full picture of a child engaged in a specific activity or at a particular learning center. Unless a teacher makes routine observation part of the daily classroom routine, observation records will likely be spotty. This can lead to misunderstandings about children's behavior or academic performance, which can be harmful to a child's self-image.

Looking, Listening, and Learning (cont.)

Connections to Standards

Teachers want to be effective, gathering rich data about children's abilities and responding to various levels of education standards. Sometimes, even the best intentions negatively impact children's learning experiences. A preschool teacher at a charter school once shared with me her concern that the school's director was using the state "guidelines" for preschool learning experiences as an assessment tool rather than for curriculum planning. Despite the document's clear statement that the guidelines were designed to focus on how teachers can help young children develop skills and knowledge and not designed to be developmental benchmarks for three- and four-year-olds, the experiences were being used as a checklist. Teachers were told to use the guidelines to evaluate children's abilities.

The teacher explained how one guideline under the Life Sciences section, which is linked to a preschool curriculum standard under "States of Matter," was being used as a checklist. Teachers were asked to check off the individual items as separate skills for each child instead of using the items as examples of experiences that help children develop the suggested skills laid out in the guideline:

- Explore, describe, and compare the properties of liquids and solids found in children's daily environment.

- Manipulate and describe materials such as water, sand, clay, and play dough.

- Explore ways materials can be changed by freezing/melting; dissolving (e.g., sugar crystals or gelatin in water); combining materials (e.g., earth + water = mud); physical force (e.g., pushing, pulling, pounding, stretching materials such as play dough or clay).

- Experiment with "magic mixtures" of common materials (e.g., flour, baking soda, cornstarch, water, salt, vinegar, food color), observe the results, then describe their experiments to others (Early Childhood Advisory Council 2003, 24).

The concern that she shared is important. It echoes a position shared by many early childhood teachers: as more time is required to teach children specific skills, less time is available for teachers to form relationships with and deep understandings of children. The benefits of documentation, including the opportunity to collaborate with children and peers, cannot be achieved with checklists.

Developmentally appropriate experiences should not be replaced with higher expectations and benchmarks that are not on par with young children's cognitive, social, and physical development. Using the example above, even if a kindergarten student is able to say what happens when vinegar is added to a baking soda mixture, he or she may not be able to use the fine-motor skills needed to successfully carry out the experiment. Instead, photographs or a running record for the time this child spends at the science center would provide more valuable information about his or her development. The more time a child spends exploring, playing, and developing self-confidence during activities like the ones that are provided in this book, the more true classroom practice is to the intention with which the experiences were designed. Through meaningful learning center activities, the foundation for children's lifetime love of learning is firmly established.

Reflection

Learning centers provide early childhood teachers opportunities to learn about their students' progress as well as their own professional and personal growth. When teachers engage in reflective practice, they observe children's learning in the moment, revisit moments of learning through the use of documentation, and plan for future classroom activities. The teacher's craft is constantly evolving in the same manner that children's learning evolves, and children and teachers become partners in the learning process. The following reflective practices represent different levels of reflection. Successful early childhood teachers engage in each level of reflection, alone and with others, to gain insights into their teaching and young children's learning.

Shallow Reflection

When teachers engage in shallow reflection, they often notice progress relating to certain goals. This is often the type of reflection that gets shared with families in the form of newsletters and bulletin boards posted inside and outside the classroom space. For example, a teacher might observe how many letters his or her preschoolers are able to recognize and then reflect on how he or she might keep students focused on the alphabet in small-group center activities. A second-grade teacher might notice that children were fidgety during a large-group discussion about the town library, and then reflect on ways to help students create a library in the Language and Literacy Center.

Applied Reflection

When teachers are able to make connections between theory and practice, they are able to make connections between their observations, educational theory, and design of new activities. For example, when a first-grade teacher uses learning centers to see what children know, want to know, and how they will go about learning something new, that teacher can observe children's learning and reflect upon his or her own success in helping students connect new information to previous knowledge. A preschool teacher might notice his or her three-year-olds getting cranky while waiting for him or her to pass out snack and reflect upon ways to provide opportunities for children to develop autonomy in the classroom.

Analytical Reflection

This type of reflection expands teachers' observations and reflections to consider issues outside their classrooms. Teachers engaged in analytical reflection recognize that their actions have consequences and that classroom practices are linked to larger social, political, and ethical issues. A preschool teacher might observe that some children get more turns at the computer than others even though they use an "eeny, meeny, miny, mo" song to choose who will go to each center. The teacher might engage the class in an activity to find an equitable, democratic practice for selecting daily learning center activities and reflect upon ways in which every child will have opportunities to make choices in the classroom. A second-grade teacher who observes students in leveled reading groups might reflect upon whether differentiated instruction within groups would provide nonnative English speakers with more opportunities for success at the learning centers. He or she might further reflect on ways to document students' successes in the classroom, and invite parent volunteers in to help take photos and record dialogue.

Self-Reflection

Putting it all together—a teacher uses the information he or she has collected and his or her awareness of the greater landscape for education to consider his or her own teaching practice. Some teachers use journals as a way to develop the habit of writing about classroom experiences. Teachers look for ways that their individual biases, beliefs, and values impact classroom practices. Such reflective practices are valuable to novice teachers as well as seasoned veterans. Many of Vivian Paley's books, such as *The Girl with the Brown Crayon* (1998), provide excellent examples of reflective practice and feature specific moments of self-reflection.

Looking and listening provide teachers and children with short- and long-term learning benefits. As a result of close observation, teachers may develop new empathy toward a specific child or a group of children. Empathy is as important for young children as it is for teachers, so modeling behaviors through the use of documentation helps create a classroom environment that is respectful to all members of the group. Inviting colleagues, parents and families, and children to be primary, active participants in classroom learning experiences establishes strong relationships that shape highly engaging classroom activities that ripple throughout the school, home environments, and broader community.

How to Use This Book

In this book, there are 70 activities that support children's learning experiences. Each unit focuses on a specific learning center and provides opportunities for integrating content areas that are often treated as exclusive domains. These activities encourage children to practice academic skills but also offer opportunities for children to learn other valuable skills such as empathy, self-regulation, responsibility for self and others, and how to participate fully and exercise basic freedoms.

The **standard** listed indicates the area of focus for each center.

The **overview** provides a quick description of what will be done in each center.

A **materials** list for each center is provided.

A **preparation note** is included for centers that require action prior to the implementation of the center.

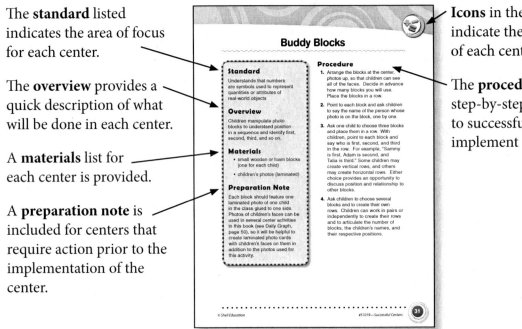

Icons in the top corners indicate the content area of each center.

The **procedure** provides step-by-step instructions to successfully implement each center.

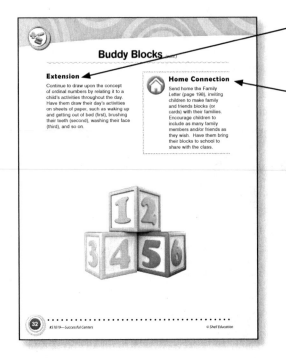

The **extension** offers opportunities to expand children's learning after completing the center.

The **home connection** allows children to deepen their learning with their families in the home.

How to Use This Book <small>(cont.)</small>

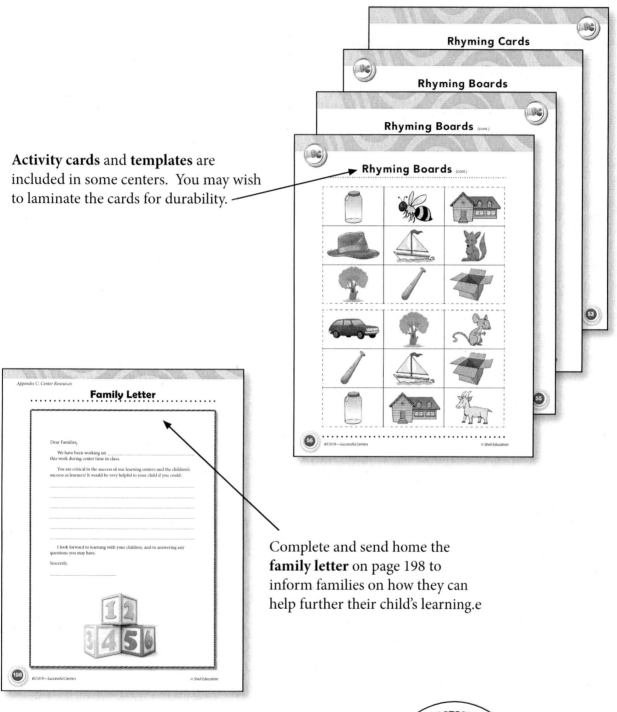

Activity cards and **templates** are included in some centers. You may wish to laminate the cards for durability.

Complete and send home the **family letter** on page 198 to inform families on how they can help further their child's learning.e

A **digital resource CD** is provided and includes resources, such as activity cards and recipes, needed to implement specific centers.

Correlation to the Standards

Shell Education is committed to producing educational materials that are research and standards based. In this effort, we have correlated all of our products to the academic standards of all 50 United States, the District of Columbia, the Department of Defense Dependent Schools, and all Canadian provinces.

How To Find Standards Correlations

To print a customized correlation report of this product for your state, visit our website at **http://www.shelleducation.com** and follow the on-screen directions. If you require assistance in printing correlation reports, please contact Customer Service at 1-877-777-3450.

Purpose and Intent of Standards

Legislation mandates that all states adopt academic standards that identify the skills students will learn in kindergarten through grade twelve. Many states also have standards for Pre–K. This same legislation sets requirements to ensure the standards are detailed and comprehensive.

Standards are designed to focus instruction and guide adoption of curricula. Standards are statements that describe the criteria necessary for students to meet specific academic goals. They define the knowledge, skills, and content students should acquire at each level. Standards are also used to develop standardized tests to evaluate students' academic progress. Teachers are required to demonstrate how their lessons meet state standards. State standards are used in the development of all of our products, so educators can be assured they meet the academic requirements of each state.

McREL Compendium

We use the Mid-continent Research for Education and Learning (McREL) Compendium to create standards correlations. Each year, McREL analyzes state standards and revises the compendium. By following this procedure, McREL is able to produce a general compilation of national standards. Each lesson in this product is based on one or more McREL standards, which are provided on the Digital Resource CD (standards.pdf).

TESOL and WIDA Standards

The lessons in this book promote English language development for English language learners. The standards correlation can be found on the digital resource CD (standards.pdf).

Standards Correlations Chart

Standard	Center(s)
Math 2.1—Understands that numbers are symbols used to represent quantities or attributes of real-world objects	Buddy Blocks (p. 31); Monkey Business (p. 33); Numbers Scavenger Hunt (p. 40)
Math 2.3—Understands symbolic, concrete, and pictorial representations of numbers	Math Stories (p. 44)
Math 3.1—Adds and subtracts whole numbers	Playful Dough (p. 36)
Math 4.3—Knows processes for telling time, counting money, and measuring length, width, height, weight, and temperature, using basic standard and non-standard units	Measuring Feet (p. 48)
Math 4.4—Makes quantitative estimates of familiar linear dimensions, weights, and time intervals and checks them against measurements	Guessing Jar (p. 45)
Math 5.1—Understands basic properties of simple geometric shapes and similarities and differences between simple geometric shapes	Secret Shape Bag (p. 42)
Math 5.4—Understands that patterns can be made by putting different shapes together or taking them apart	Pattern House (p. 39)
Math 6.1—Collects and represents information about objects or events in simple graphs	Daily Graph (p. 50)
Language Arts 1.1—Knows that writing, including pictures, letters, and words, communicates meaning and information	Story Rocks (p. 78); Gratitude Letters (p. 190)
Language Arts 1.3—Uses forms of emergent writing	Scribble Stories (p. 72)
Language Arts 1.6—Uses writing and other methods to describe familiar persons, places, objects, or experiences	Once Upon a Time (p. 68); Tall Tales (p. 74)

Standards Correlations Chart *(cont.)*

Standard	Center(s)
Language Arts 1.8—Writes for different purposes	How-to Books (p. 76)
Language Arts 3.1—Uses conventions of print in writing	The Daily News (p. 63)
Language Arts 5.9—Knows all uppercase and lowercase letters of the alphabet	Say It With Dough (p. 58)
Language Arts 6.2—Knows setting, main characters, main events, sequence, narrator, and problems in stories	Puppet Stories (p. 66)
Language Arts 8.5—Uses level-appropriate vocabulary in speech	Add a Word (p. 57)
Language Arts 8.16—Knows rhyming sounds and simple rhymes	Rhyming Board (p. 52)
Science 1.1—Knows that short-term weather conditions can change daily, and weather patterns can change over seasons	Weather Wheels (p. 89)
Science 2.1—Knows that Earth materials consist of solid rocks, soils, liquid water, and the gases of the atmosphere	Private Beach (p. 189)
Science 12.1—Uses the senses to make observations about living things, nonliving objects, and events	Just the Right Mix (p. 81); Nature Mural (p. 95); Listening Jars (p. 97); Rainbow Sculptures (p. 185); Some Sort of Garden (p. 188)
Science 12.1—Knows that learning can come from careful observations and simple experiments	Magic Messages (p. 85); Egg Float (p. 86); Find the Baby (p. 93) Balancing Act (p. 99)
Science 12.2—Knows that tools can be used to gather information and extend the senses	Texture Projector (p. 83)
Science 12.3—Makes predictions based on patterns	Shadow Sketches (p. 91)

#51019—Successful Centers

Standards Correlations Chart *(cont.)*

Standard	Center(s)
Social Studies 1.1—Understands that maps can represent his or her surroundings	A Room of My Own (p. 117); My School (p. 130)
Social Studies 1.1—Understands the globe as a representation of the Earth	Where Would I Build a Home? (p. 132)
Social Studies 1.2—Knows how to develop picture time lines of their own lives or their family's history	Family and Friends Time Lines (p. 119); Photo Diaries (p. 121)
Social Studies 1.6—Knows ways in which people share family beliefs and values	Time Capsule (p. 123)
Social Studies 3.1—Understands rules and the purposes they serve	Exercise Your Rights (p. 128)
Social Studies 4.4—Knows how different groups of people in the community have taken responsibility for the common good	Community Workers (p. 125)
Social Studies 7.2—Knows the holidays and ceremonies of different societies	Calendar Collage (p. 102)
Economics 3.1—Knows that a price is the amount of money that people pay when they buy a good or service	Classroom Bank (p. 134)
Visual Arts 1.1—Experiments with a variety of color, textures, and shapes	Color Dance (p. 137); My City, Your City (p. 144); Texture Pizza (p. 149); Blot a Lot (p. 151); What Would Happen If…? (p. 154)
Visual Arts 1.3—Knows the similarities and differences in the meanings of common terms used in various arts	Let's Take a Line Walk (p. 147)
Visual Arts 2.3—Uses visual structures and functions to communicate ideas	Color My Mood (p. 146); Scrappy Books (p. 153)

Standards Correlations Chart *(cont.)*

Standard	Center(s)
Dance 1.1—Moves his or her body in a variety of controlled ways	Mirror Me (p. 139); 1, 2, 3…Do the Freeze! (p. 170)
Theatre 3.1—Creates props to support dramatic play	Craft Stick Puppets (p. 142)
Music 2.1—Echoes short rhythms and melodic patterns	Shake It Up (p. 157); Match My Moves (p. 159); Sentence Sonata (p. 161)
Music 4.1—Knows the source of a variety of sounds	Musical Instrument Medley (p. 165); Soft Symphony (p. 167); Name that Instrument! (p. 169)
Music 4.1—Uses a variety of sound sources when composing	Musical Jars (p. 168)
Music 5.1—Knows standard symbols used to notate meter, rhythm, pitch, and dynamics in simple patterns	Super Sheet Music (p. 162)
Music 7.1—Knows that music comes from different places and different periods of time	Dance Around the World (p. 166)
Thinking and Reasoning 3.1—Identifies the similarities and differences between persons, places, things, and events using concrete data	Superheroes (p. 172); Travel Grab Bags (p. 187)
Thinking and Reasoning 5.1—Identifies simple problems and possible solutions	Big Store (p. 174)
Health 4.1—Identifies and shares feelings in appropriate ways	Feelings Cards (p. 178)
Health 5.2—Knows safe behaviors in the classroom and on the playground	Safety Bingo (p. 180)
Health 6.1—Classifies foods and food combinations according to the food groups	Food for Thought (p. 176)

Standards Correlations Chart *(cont.)*

Standard	Center(s)
TESOL/WIDA Standard 1—English language learners communicate for **Social** and **Instructional** purposes within the school setting	All Centers
TESOL/WIDA Standard 2—English language learners communicate information, ideas, and concepts necessary for academic success in the content area of **Language Arts**	All Centers
TESOL/WIDA Standard 3—English language learners communicate information, ideas, and concepts necessary for academic success in the content area of **Mathematics**	All Math Centers (pp. 31–50)
TESOL/WIDA Standard 4—English language learners communicate information, ideas, and concepts necessary for academic success in the content area of **Science**	All Science Centers (pp. 81–99)
TESOL/WIDA Standard 5—English language learners communicate information, ideas, and concepts necessary for academic success in the content area of **Social Studies**	All Social Studies Centers (pp. 102–135)

Math Centers

It is impossible to be a mathematician without being a poet in soul.

—Sophia Kovalevskaya (1850–1891)

Math learning centers are areas within the classroom where children may work alone, with a partner, or in small groups to use materials designed to expand their mathematical thinking. The activities reinforce classroom curriculum and prior instruction and provide authentic opportunities for children to practice problem solving, reasoning, and communicating mathematical knowledge. The teacher is able to observe and interact with children during the activities, and the nature of the task will indicate the level of support the teacher needs to provide. Depending on the age and abilities of the children, activities can be modified to challenge children's thinking. For example, some children may stretch their thinking to re-create teacher-created patterns, while other children may design their own patterns. Duplicate stations may be helpful to manage the number of students interested in participating on a given day, and computer resources (e.g., Internet, software) can complement Math Center activities. The 10 activities in this section integrate math with language and literacy, art, music, and science. Many of the ideas can be extended and revisited in different learning centers.

Buddy Blocks

Standard

Understands that numbers are symbols used to represent quantities or attributes of real-world objects

Overview

Children manipulate photo blocks to understand position in a sequence and identify first, second, third, and so on.

Materials

- small wooden or foam blocks (one for each child)
- children's photos (laminated)

Preparation Note

Each block should feature one laminated photo of one child in the class glued to one side. Photos of children's faces can be used in several center activities in this book (see Daily Graph, page 50), so it will be helpful to create laminated photo cards with children's faces on them in addition to the photos used for this activity.

Procedure

1. Arrange the blocks at the center, photos up, so that children can see all of the faces. Decide in advance how many blocks you will use. Place the blocks in a row.

2. Point to each block and ask children to say the name of the person whose photo is on the block, one by one.

3. Ask one child to choose three blocks and place them in a row. With children, point to each block and say who is first, second, and third in the row. For example, "Sammy is first, Adam is second, and Talia is third." Some children may create vertical rows, and others may create horizontal rows. Either choice provides an opportunity to discuss position and relationship to other blocks.

4. Ask children to choose several blocks and to create their own rows. Children can work in pairs or independently to create their rows and to articulate the number of blocks, the children's names, and their respective positions.

Buddy Blocks *(cont.)*

Extension

Continue to draw upon the concept of ordinal numbers by relating it to a child's activities throughout the day. Have them draw their day's activities on sheets of paper, such as waking up and getting out of bed (first), brushing their teeth (second), washing their face (third), and so on.

Home Connection

Send home the Family Letter (page 198), inviting children to make family and friends blocks (or cards) with their families. Encourage children to include as many family members and/or friends as they wish. Have them bring their blocks to school to share with the class.

Monkey Business

Standard

Understands that numbers are symbols used to represent quantities or attributes of real-world objects

Overview

Children participate in singing a familiar song that associates specific numbers with concrete actions.

Materials

- "Five Little Monkeys" Lyrics (page 35)

- manipulatives (e.g., plastic monkeys, counters)

Procedure

1. Teach children the lyrics to "Five Little Monkeys." This song is also available in a children's book (or lends itself nicely to the creation of overhead slides) that can be used in the Language and Literacy Center and/or a large-group activity.

2. Sing the song together with a small group of children, picking up one of the manipulatives each time the song calls for one monkey to be falling off the bed. Use gestures to illustrate other parts of the song, such as pretending to pick up and dial a phone and/or wagging a pointer finger admonishingly during "No more monkeys jumping on the bed!"

3. Sing the song all the way through, and invite children to take turns picking up the manipulatives each time. They may also make predictions about what will happen next.

Monkey Business *(cont.)*

Extension

Ask children to decide upon other manipulatives to use in this game, and to change the song accordingly. For example, children might choose "apples" instead of monkeys, "tree" instead of bed, and "knee" instead of head. Remember that rhyming isn't the important piece in this exercise—the focus here is on counting.

Home Connection

Send home the "Five Little Monkeys" Lyrics (page 35) and the Family Letter (page 198), asking children to do this activity with their families. You may wish to include some of the alternative words that children came up with during the extension to provide examples for families.

"Five Little Monkeys" Lyrics

Five little monkeys, jumping on the bed.

One fell off and bumped his head.

Mama called the doctor and the doctor said,

"No more monkeys jumping on the bed!"

(repeat above with four, three, two, one monkey, and then the final verse)

No little monkeys, jumping on the bed.

None fell off and bumped his head.

Mama called the doctor, and the doctor said,

"Put those monkeys back in their bed!"

Playful Dough

Standard

Adds and subtracts whole numbers

Overview

Children use play dough to practice simple addition and subtraction.

Materials

- play dough (store-bought or from recipe on page 38)
- placemat or tray (one per child)
- whiteboard

Preparation Note

If you would like to make your own play dough instead of using store-bought, gather the ingredients from the play dough recipe (page 38). You may wish to make it in front of children to have an added math connection of measurement.

Procedure

1. Tell children that they will create addition and/or subtraction problems using the dough. Distribute parts of the play dough to children. Ask them to divide their dough into 10 small balls. You may wish to do this for them depending on children's abilities.

2. Write the first number of a simple addition or subtraction problem on the board. As you write it, say the number aloud and have children place the same number of play dough balls out in front of them. Ask them to count their play dough balls to make sure they have the correct amount.

3. Tell children whether they will be adding to or subtracting from to the amount of play dough in front of them. Then say the second number of the problem. Children should add more play dough balls to the amount if it is an addition problem or take away play dough balls if it is a subtraction problem.

4. Allow children to count their play dough balls after they have completed the problems. Have them discuss their answers with the group.

Playful Dough *(cont.)*

Extension

Have children write simple addition and subtraction problems such as 2 + 2 = 4 and 5 − 3 = 2 on index cards or sheets of paper. Have them use the balls of play dough to represent the equations.

Home Connection

Send home the Family Letter (page 198) and the play dough recipe (page 38) to families. Encourage them to make the play dough at home. Ask families to create simple problems for their children to solve.

Play Dough Recipe

Ingredients:

- $1\frac{1}{2}$ C water
- 3 C flour
- $\frac{1}{2}$ C salt
- $\frac{1}{4}$ C oil
- Food coloring

Directions:

1. In a large bowl, mix together ingredients.

2. Knead dough with hands to reach desired consistency.

3. Divide dough into portions. You may wish to use food coloring during this activity to achieve desired colors.

Note: Be aware of children's allergies prior to having them work with the play dough.

#51019—Successful Centers

Pattern House

Standard

Understands that patterns can be made by putting different shapes together or taking them apart

Overview

Children use patterns to decorate paper bag houses.

Materials

- index cards
- small stickers in familiar shapes (e.g., circles, stars, flowers)
- construction paper
- paper bags
- markers and crayons

Preparation Notes

- Cut construction paper into rectangular shapes for windows and doors.
- Prepare paper bag "houses" in advance by cutting the tops of the paper bags into points for the roofs.
- Prepare index cards with sample patterns on them, such as *red circle*, *blue circle*, *red circle*, *blue circle*.

Procedure

1. Show children the pattern examples. Explain to them what a pattern is and that they will use different patterns to create houses of thier own. Invite children to begin with creating windows and doors by gluing the rectangular pieces of construction paper to the bags. Have them use stickers or markers to create patterns on the sides of the houses.

2. Ask children to discuss the patterns that they chose to create on their houses. Children can write or dictate a sentence about their houses.

3. When children have finished, set aside a time for an "open house" large-group activity in which children "visit" each others' houses and examine the different patterns.

Extension

Have children re-create patterns with concrete objects such as beads, colored cubes, and buttons.

 ## Home Connection

Send home the Family Letter (page 198), asking families to look for patterns around their homes. You may wish to have children take photos of the patterns to share with the class.

Numbers Scavenger Hunt

Standard

Understands that numbers are symbols used to represent quantities or attributes of real-world objects

Overview

Children locate specific quantities of objects in the classroom.

Materials

- Numbers Scavenger Hunt (page 41)
- clipboards
- pencils

Procedure

1. Explain to children that numbers can be represented with objects around the classroom. Share examples, noting the features of each representation (e.g., 3, ***, flower with 3 petals).

2. Provide children with Numbers Scavenger Hunt sheets on clipboards. Have them work independently or with partners to find each number represented in the classroom (e.g., number of tables, stripes on a rug, dots on upholstery, floor tiles).

3. Children will hunt for objects in the classroom to match the numbers on their Numbers Scavenger Hunt sheets, and draw the object(s) in the box. When children complete their sheets they may choose to write a sentence using a number word.

Extension

Provide children with pictures of objects found in nature, and ask them to glue the pictures as representations on square sheets of paper. Have them write the amount pictured of the object(s). Students' papers can be assembled into a class number "quilt."

Home Connection

Send home the Numbers Scavenger Hunt sheet (page 41) and the Family Letter (page 198), explaining how to use the Numbers Scavenger Hunt sheet. Encourage families to go on hunts in their homes.

Numbers Scavenger Hunt

Name: _____ **Date:** _____

Directions: Read the numbers below. Look for that amount of an object. Then draw the object in the box.

1	2	3
4	5	6
7	8	9

   #51019—Successful Centers

Secret Shape Bag

Standard

Understands basic properties of simple geometric shapes and similarities and differences between simple geometric shapes

Overview

Children take turns reaching into a bag, selecting one object, and attempting to identify the object based on its attributes.

Materials

- shape manipulatives (e.g., tangram shapes, square beads, circular discs)
- small- to medium-sized paper or cloth bag
- cloth blindfold (optional)

Procedure

1. Show objects to children. Allow children to discuss each object. Then, place objects into the Secret Shape Bag. You may wish to have the children place the objects in the bag.

2. Instruct a child to wear a blindfold or to close his or her eyes if the child is uncomfortable with the blindfold and select one object from the bag and to pull it out so the group can see it. Ask the other children in the group to refrain from talking to the child.

3. Ask the child who selected the object to describe what the shape feels like, noting the features of the shape. For example, he or she might say how many corners the object has or how many flat surfaces there are.

4. Prompt the child to make an informed guess about what shape it is. If the child guesses correctly, place the shape on the table and pass the bag to the next child. If the child guesses incorrectly, place the shape back in the bag, and pass the bag to the next child. Continue playing until all of the shapes have been removed from the bag and identified correctly.

Secret Shape Bag *(cont.)*

Extension

Focus on one shape and provide multiple objects that are all the same shape (e.g., circular objects such as buttons, coins, or lids from jars). Discuss how each object is the specified shape.

Home Connection

Send home the Family Letter (page 198), inviting children to bring in one small object from home to add to the Secret Shape Bag.

Math Stories

Standard

Understands symbolic, concrete, and pictorial representations of numbers

Overview

Children use a felt board and felt shapes to tell a math story.

Materials

- felt board with inviting background (e.g., beach: water, sand, sun; space: stars, moon)

- felt shapes that correspond to the theme of the felt background (e.g., beach: seashells, fish, crabs; space: planets, rockets)

Procedure

1. Model for children by starting a math story such as, "I went to the beach and I saw *two red crabs* crawling on the sand." Place two felt crabs on the felt board.

2. Invite children to take turns placing items on the felt board and to narrate the story as they select felt items. Remind them to use numbers in their stories.

3. When all items are on the felt board and their stories have been told, children may choose a different background and start again with a new math story.

Extension

When all items are on the felt board within one math storyline, begin to subtract items, articulating the movement in such a way as, "I left the circus, and I took home *three lions*." The felt board can be made available in other centers as well, such as the Language and Literacy Center and the Art Center.

 ## Home Connection

Send home the Family Letter (page 198), encouraging children to tell math stories with their families at home. Invite family members to come to class and share a math story using objects from their respective home environments.

Guessing Jar

Standard

Makes quantitative estimates of familiar linear dimensions, weights, and time intervals and checks them against measurements

Overview

Children observe small objects and estimate how many items are in a jar and compare the actual number with their guesses.

Materials

- multiple small objects (e.g., buttons, pennies, plastic toys, plastic jewels, marbles)

- large clear jar with lid

- Guessing Sheet (page 47)

Procedure

1. Place 5 to 20 of the same object in the Guessing Jar. Have children draw the object in the first column of the Guessing Sheet.

2. Instruct children to look carefully at the Guessing Jar and guess how many objects are in the jar. Have them record their guesses in the second column of the Guessing Sheet. You may wish to have children write or draw their guesses.

3. When all children have recorded their guesses, help them, as needed, to open the jar and count the actual number of objects in the jar. Children may work alone, with a partner, or with the center group.

4. Ask children to write or draw the actual number of objects on the Guessing Sheets. Have them discuss the results with the group.

#51019—Successful Centers

Guessing Jar *(cont.)*

Extension

Children can be asked to estimate larger numbers of smaller objects and to write down their guesses on their Guessing Sheets. They can also create their own tiny objects to place in the Guessing Jar. After they have developed a strong sense of how to estimate and count the number of objects, they can be encouraged to represent the difference between the guess and the actual number, and to learn math vocabulary such as *more than* and *less than*.

Home Connection

Send home the Family Letter (page 198), asking each child to bring in a small number of objects from home to place in the Guessing Jar. Children can take turns sharing their objects with the class or respective center group.

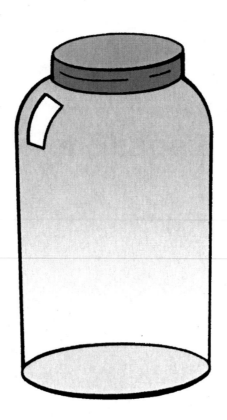

Guessing Sheet

Name: _____ Date: _____

Directions: Draw the object from the jar. Write how many objects you think are in the jar. Count the objects. Then write the actual number of objects.

Object	My Guess	Actual Number

© Shell Education   #51019—Successful Centers

Measuring Feet

Standard

Knows processes for telling time, counting money, and measuring length, width, height, weight, and temperature, using basic standard and non-standard units

Overview

Children determine the length of a line using their own feet as units of measurement and discuss how different-size feet impact their answers relating to length.

Materials

- masking tape
- chart paper or chalkboard/dry-erase board
- yardstick
- ruler

Procedure

1. Explain to children that you want to figure out the length of one part of the room/floor.

2. Using masking tape, create a line on the floor, approximately 6 feet long. Ask children to take turns walking along the line, step by step, as the group counts the number of steps each child takes. You may wish to model how to walk with your heel touching the top of your toe to obtain a correct measurement. Keep track of the number of footsteps each child takes on chart paper or a chalkboard/dry-erase board.

3. As a group, compare the outcomes, noting different numbers of footsteps that were required for each child to walk from one end of the line to the other. Ask children to share their ideas about why the numbers were different or similar. Explain that the numbers are different because the sizes of their feet are not the same (non-standard unit of measurement). Tell children that if they had used a ruler, the measurements would have been the same because all rulers have the same length (standard unit of measurement).

Extension

Share different standard units of measurement with children, such as a yardstick or a ruler, noting what one inch looks like on each tool. Instruct children to use the ruler and yardstick to measure the line of tape and compare the outcomes.

Home Connection

Send home the Family Letter (page 198), encouraging children to work with their families to measure furniture, rugs, or other items in their homes, using creative units of measurement or standard units of measurement found on rulers, yardsticks, and measuring tapes.

Daily Graph

Standard

Collects and represents information about objects or events in simple graphs

Overview

Children use photo cards to represent a choice and create an instant visual representation of data.

Materials

- pocket chart
- child photos (laminated)

Preparation Note

Laminate a photo of each child.

Procedure

1. Place a question or other prompt in the pocket chart, such as *What is your favorite color?,* in the Math Center. Choices for responses should be placed along the left-hand side, such as *Red, Blue, Pink, Green,* and *Other.*

2. Explain to children that they will select their own answers to the question and once they have done so, they may interview other children in the group to find out their responses. Have them place children's photo cards in the pocket chart slots accordingly.

3. Have children discuss the results as a group.

Extension

Older children may use comparative vocabulary to describe the responses, such as *most* children chose _____, *many* children chose _____, *several* children chose _____, *fewer* children chose _____, _____ was chosen *least,* and so on.

Home Connection

Send home the Family Letter (page 198), inviting children to interview family members and create their own miniature graphs to represent family members' choices in response to a question or a prompt.

Language and Literacy Centers

Once you learn to read, you will be forever free.

—Frederick Douglass (1818–1895)

Language and Literacy learning centers promote success in a variety of curriculum areas related to print and communication. For example, the 10 activities in this section present opportunities for children to be exposed to oral and print materials, and to practice their own reading and writing skills in meaningful ways, alone and with peers. Similar to the teacher's role in Math Center activities (and all classroom learning centers), the teacher here is an active participant and observer, responding to children and extending action, as needed, to enrich learning experiences. Teachers can use common pieces of classroom furniture such as an easel and a pocket chart to organize the activities that follow. Many of the ideas integrate content areas such as art, science, and music.

Rhyming Board

Standard

Knows rhyming sounds and simple rhymes

Overview

Children draw a card from a pile and match the card to a corresponding image on a board based on rhyming.

Materials

- Rhyming Cards (page 53)
- Rhyming Boards (pages 54–56)
- game markers (e.g., buttons, pennies)

Preparation Note

Make copies of and cut out the Rhyming Cards (one set per group) and Rhyming Boards (one board per child).

Procedure

1. Explain to children that they will play a rhyming game. Begin by showing a card and naming the picture. Have children look on their Rhyming Boards for a picture that rhymes with the card chosen.

2. Have children take turns drawing cards and naming the objects on the cards aloud as they look for a match. Have the group place markers on the rhyming picture on their Rhyming Boards.

3. Children should continue until all of the cards are used to match items on their Rhyming Boards. Comment on the rhyming pairs that children have identified.

Extension

Have children use the Rhyming Card Template found on the Digital Resource CD (filename: rhymingcardstemplate.pdf) to draw their own rhyming cards. Put children in pairs and ask them to play Memory. They can place all of their cards facedown and take turns flipping them over to create a match.

Home Connection

Send home the Family Letter (page 198) inviting children to notice rhyming objects at home and to share them with the class.

Rhyming Cards

Rhyming Boards

Rhyming Boards *(cont.)*

Rhyming Boards (cont.)

Add a Word

Overview

Children pass around objects and take turns saying describing words for each object.

Materials

- cloth or paper bag
- small objects (e.g., paper clip, seashell, wooden block)

Procedure

1. Children take turns selecting one item from the Add a Word Bag. The first child picks one object from the bag and says one word to describe it. For example, a child who chooses a paper clip may say, "shiny."

2. The paper clip gets passed to the next child, who adds a new word to describe the object and says them both (*shiny*, *small*).

3. Once every child has had a chance to hold and describe the object, the process begins again with a different child selecting a new object from the bag.

4. Children who are working alone may choose objects and write a list of descriptors or dictate a list of words to a teacher.

Extension

Children can identify and describe all of the objects and separate them into categories based on characteristics they choose. The teacher can create Add a Word Bags based on particular themes to support content or curriculum.

Home Connection

Send home the Family Letter (page 198), encouraging children to practice their descriptors with family members, using objects they find at home. Children can also create their own Add a Word Bags in school and bring them home.

Say It With Dough

Standard

Knows all uppercase and lowercase letters of the alphabet

Overview

Children use play dough to "write" letters and words.

Materials

- Alphabet Cards (pages 59–61)
- play dough (store-bought or from recipe on page 62)

Preparation Notes

- Make copies of and cut out the Alphabet Cards. You may wish to laminate them for durability.
- Place several portions of play dough at the center.

Procedure

1. Have children explore the dough, practicing rolling the dough into "snakes" or long pieces.

2. Tell children to place the play dough on an Alphabet Card, molding the dough to cover the letters on the cards. Children who know how to form the alphabet letters can create their own free-form letters or words on the table.

3. Have children name each letter and a word that begins with that letter as they work.

Extension

Challenge children to create words with the play dough. They can use metal or plastic alphabet stamps to stamp letters into the dough to experiment with word formation. They may also enjoy pressing dry alphabet pasta or letter beads into the dough.

Home Connection

Send home the Family Letter (page 198) to share ideas with families about ways to use alphabet play at home. Play dough can be prepared in class and sent home in small plastic bags for families to enjoy creating letters and words with their children.

Alphabet Cards

A

B

C

D

E

F

G

H

I

Alphabet Cards

J	K	L
M	N	O
P	Q	R

Alphabet Cards

S	**T**	**U**
V	**W**	**X**
Y	**Z**	

Play Dough Recipe

Ingredients:

- $1\frac{1}{2}$ C water
- 3 C flour
- $\frac{1}{2}$ C salt
- $\frac{1}{4}$ C oil
- Food coloring

Directions:

1. In a large bowl, mix together ingredients.

2. Knead dough with hands to reach desired consistency.

3. Divide dough into portions. You may wish to use food coloring during this activity to achieve desired colors.

Note: Be aware of children's allergies prior to having them work with the play dough.

The Daily News

Standard

Uses conventions of print in writing

Overview

Children create group news articles that will be shared in a classroom newspaper.

Materials

- News Article (page 65)
- newspaper
- paper
- pencils
- scissors
- camera (optional)

Preparation Notes

- Examine newspapers with children during a large-group time, noticing different parts of an article such as headlines, pictures, captions, and stories.

- Create a name for the class newspaper.

Procedure

1. Invite children to create a class newspaper. Explain that each group at the center will work together to create an article that will be placed in the classroom newspaper.

2. Talk with children about ideas for a news story. Encourage children to write and/or illustrate stories on the News Article sheet. You may wish to have children dictate their stories. Children may also use a camera to take pictures instead of drawing them.

3. When stories have been completed, children can lay out the stories on sheets of paper, like a typical newspaper. Using a photocopier, reduce the size of the written stories as needed to create a class newspaper. If the stories have been dictated, the teacher-written text can be typed as needed and formatted accordingly.

The Daily News *(cont.)*

Extension

Children can be assigned specific jobs such as reporter (e.g., sports, fashion), photographer, and editor. The class can visit a local newspaper office or printing facility and speak with people who work on newspaper production. You may also wish to have an employee from the local newspaper office come visit the class to explain his or her job.

Home Connection

Send home the Family Letter (page 198), encouraging families to read appropriate newspaper articles with their children. Families can cut out interesting stories and share them with the class.

News Article

Name: _____ **Date:** _____

Puppet Stories

Standard

Knows setting, main characters, main events, sequence, narrator, and problems in stories

Overview

Children create their own puppets and stories.

Materials

- cardboard box (optional)
- paper bags
- socks
- paper for cutting
- chenille sticks
- buttons
- yarn
- glue
- scissors

Preparation Note

Create a puppet theater scene for children to use as they play with their puppets. You may wish to use a large cardboard box and cut out a frame for the stage.

Procedure

1. Explain to children that they will make puppets to use in a class Puppet Story. Introduce them to the various materials they may use to create their puppets. Help them brainstorm ideas for characters they will create.

2. Have children play around with the materials before gluing them to the sock or bag.

3. When children have finished making their puppets, invite them to imagine their Puppet Stories and practice with a friend or two. Encourage children to contribute ideas or suggestions for friends' stories.

4. When children are ready to share their Puppet Stories, invite other children to the Language and Literacy Center to enjoy the show, or dedicate a large-group time to enjoy several Puppet Stories.

Puppet Stories *(cont.)*

Extension

Make the puppets available for play in different learning centers, such as the music or art centers, so that children can use them in spontaneous play. Introduce store-bought puppets or other ones made by children or teachers to extend the play.

Home Connection

Send home the Family Letter (page 198), providing simple instructions and suggested materials for families on how they can create their own puppets at home. Invite families to share their puppets with the class.

Once Upon a Time

Standard

Uses writing and other methods to describe familiar persons, places, objects, or experiences

Overview

Children select two characters and create a story about the adventures that these characters would have.

Materials

- Character Sheet (page 70)
- Storyboard (page 71)
- paper
- pencils
- markers

Preparation Note

Make copies of the Character Sheet and cut them apart. You may wish to laminate them for durability.

Procedure

1. Discuss with children the different features of a story (setting, characters, problem, and solution). Explain that they will create their own stories.

2. Have children look at the different characters and select two characters to put in their stories. Tell them to think about how they can use the characters in a story before selecting both characters.

3. Prompt children's thinking by asking, "What would happen if these two met one day?," "What would these two do together if they had their own adventure?," and "Where would these two like to go?"

4. Distribute the Storyboard to each child. Older children may choose to write and illustrate their own stories, while younger children may dictate their stories to the teacher, perhaps adding illustrations.

5. Children can share their stories with one another during a subsequent center time or large-group activity.

Once Upon a Time (cont.)

Extension

Have children act out their stories in small groups. Once all stories have been acted out, have a discussion with children on how some stories were similar and how they were different.

 ## Home Connection

Send home the Family Letter (page 198), asking children to share the stories they created with their families. You may also suggest that the family gets together to act out the story.

Character Sheet

Storyboard

Name: _____ **Date:** _____

Directions: Plan your story by filling out the boxes below.

Setting	Characters
Problem	**Solution**

Scribble Stories

Standard

Uses forms of emergent writing

Overview

Children take turns scribbling on paper and turning the scribbles into illustrations that inspire stories.

Materials

- paper
- pencils
- gentle bell
- crayons
- colored markers

Procedure

1. Explain to children that they will have a few seconds to scribble on their papers and then they will use those papers to create their own stories.

2. Start the activity by saying, "Scribble me a story!" and making a sound using a soft bell or other gentle musical sound. After five to ten seconds, repeat the sound and ask children to put down their pencils. **Note:** If children are alone at the center, assign a "scribble starter" and an order so that all group members can have a turn.

3. Instruct children to look at their papers and to think about what their scribbles remind them of or resemble. Children can add lines to the scribbles as needed to complete an idea or image and then should draw other elements that lend themselves to the stories that are coming to mind.

4. When children have finished their drawings, they can take turns telling their stories to the group.

Scribble Stories *(cont.)*

Extension

Older children may work together to create one longer story, with each illustration representing one chapter or event in a sequence. Children may write the words to their stories, use a computer to type their stories, or ask a teacher to write the words for them. Children can exchange scribbles so that each scribbler receives someone else's scribble to turn into a story. Depending on the children's interests or a theme the class is studying, the teacher can instruct children to focus on the same topic as they scribble and generate stories.

Home Connection

Send home the Family Letter (page 198), encouraging children to scribble stories at home with their families. Children may choose to bring in scribble stories from home to share with the class. You may wish to create a scribble binder for all scribble stories brought in from children's homes.

Tall Tales

Standard

Uses writing and other methods to describe familiar persons, places, objects, or experiences

Overview

Children use rolls of paper to write stories and add to existing stories over time.

Materials

- rolls of adding-machine/ receipt paper
- pencils
- markers
- clothes hangers (optional)
- string (optional)

Preparation Note

Create a story on adding-machine/receipt paper several feet long to provide as an example for children.

Procedure

1. Share your example of a story that is several feet of paper long, reading from left to right, beginning to end. Ask children if the story sounds true or not true and how they came up with their decision. Discuss features of the story that show fiction and nonfiction.

2. Instruct children to use the adding-machine/receipt paper to write words or draw pictures that tell a story about something of interest. **Note:** You may wish to demonstrate a suggested length to children to avoid excessive use of paper.

3. Stories can be stored on clothes hangers or loops of string for easy access and enjoyment by peers.

Tall Tales *(cont.)*

Extension

Children can learn more about tall tales, such as those written about Paul Bunyan or Davy Crockett, and discuss the elements of American tall tales. Older children can create and describe results of their research through drawings, paintings, photographs, and/or new stories.

Home Connection

Send home the Family Letter (page 198), asking family members to write down family stories or legends that were shared when they were children and to share them with the class through email or by sending them in with the children.

How-to Books

Standard

Writes for different purposes

Overview

Children create a unique book that describes how to do something.

Materials

- paper
- pencils
- crayons
- colored markers

Procedure

1. Introduce this activity to children by sharing with them something that you do well or know much about. For example, a teacher might say that he or she knows how to bake delicious bread and then briefly describe the steps needed to make, bake, and eat the bread.

2. Ask children to think about something they know how to do and really enjoy doing. Ask them how they would help a friend learn how to do it. If children struggle to identify something, suggest favorite activities that they often engage in at school or at home. Children can take turns sharing some ideas about what they know how to do.

3. Provide children with paper and writing or coloring materials. Younger children can draw pictures and dictate their instructions to a teacher, while older children may wish to write their own instructions.

How-to Books *(cont.)*

Extension

When children have finished their How-to Books, they can share them with a friend to "test" the instructions and to see how they might modify some words, illustrations, or steps to better help someone learn and execute the process.

Home Connection

Send home the Family Letter (page 198), inviting families into the classroom for a "How-to Party" to celebrate all of the children as experts. Have the How-to Books on display for families to enjoy.

Story Rocks

Standard

Knows that writing, including pictures, letters, and words, communicates meaning and information

Overview

Children create Story Rocks that represent elements of a story and prompt connections to other stories and dramatic play

Materials

- small round or oval stones that have smooth surfaces

- magazines with colorful illustrations and images

- colored paper

- scissors

- $\frac{1}{2}$ glue and $\frac{1}{2}$ water mixture (or Mod Podge®)

- paintbrushes

Preparation Note

You may wish to preselect and precut magazine images for children.

Procedure

1. Present materials at the center to children. Explain that they will create their own Story Rocks to tell stories that they imagine.

2. Ask children to select 1–2 smooth rocks and then choose pictures from magazines that have been cut out in advance, or they can cut out their own pictures or designs from magazines. Some children may wish to cut pieces of colored paper into small pieces that can be used to construct characters or objects to be glued onto the rocks.

3. Have children glue the materials onto the rocks. Then have them brush a top layer of glue over the materials.

4. When the Story Rocks are dry, children can take turns telling their own stories, using their rocks as prompts.

Story Rocks *(cont.)*

Extension

Story Rocks can be sorted into themes, such as animals and cars, and stored together. Children can take turns contributing to one longer story. Teachers can create surprise Story Rocks that add new elements or twists to favorite stories or themes.

Home Connection

Send home the Family Letter (page 198), encouraging children to tell their stories to their families. Have families work together to search for smooth, small rocks near their homes or when visiting other places with their families to contribute rocks to the Story Rock supply collection.

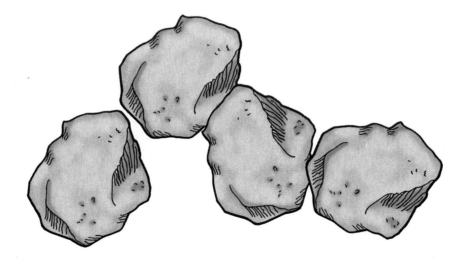

Science Centers

Every great advance in science has issued from a new audacity of imagination.

—John Dewey (1929)

Science learning centers provide children with a wide range of opportunities to observe, develop and test hypotheses and follow their natural curiosities. Through hands-on experiences with objects and through simple experiments, children learn to measure, classify, make inferences, and communicate their findings with peers and adults. The teacher is able to enhance children's experiences with common objects found in nature, such as leaves, flowers, rocks, and shells. Manmade materials, such as measuring tools, magnifying glasses, and pulleys expose children to new qualities and characteristics that they can explore alone and with others. The 10 activities in this section present children with concrete experiences that promote critical-thinking tools to help them make sense of the world in new and meaningful ways.

Just the Right Mix

Standard

Uses the senses to make observations about living things, nonliving objects, and events

Overview

Children explore how their actions and materials impact the experiment.

Materials

- empty clear plastic water bottle(s)
- measuring cups
- water
- food coloring
- cooking oil (corn or vegetable)
- dish soap

Preparation Note

Prepare water bottles with $\frac{1}{4}$ cup of water in them. Children may work alone or with a partner, so it may be helpful to have several bottles ready at the start of learning center time.

Procedure

1. Distribute a water bottle to each child or pair. Invite children to add a few drops of food coloring to their water bottles. Have them seal the lid tightly and shake the closed bottles to mix the water and food coloring. Have children observe what happens.

2. Have them seal the lid tightly and shake the closed bottles to mix the water and food coloring. Add $\frac{1}{4}$ cup of cooking oil to each of the bottles. Be sure children put the caps back on securely. Ask children to look carefully at the water and oil and to describe what the liquid looks like. Invite children to shake their closed bottles again. **Note:** The water and oil might appear to blend together but will quickly separate, with the oil resting on top of the water.

3. Ask children to predict what will happen if dish soap is added to the liquids in their bottles. Squirt some dish soap into the water bottles and see what happens when the children shake their bottles once they are closed tightly. Discuss whether or not their predictions were accurate.

Just the Right Mix *(cont.)*

Extension

Do a similar experiment with ground black pepper, water, and dish soap. Pour an inch of water into a pie pan or shallow dish, and sprinkle black pepper on the water. Ask children to predict what will happen if a drop of dish soap is added to the water, and then see what happens.

 ## Home Connection

Send home the Family Letter (page 198), asking children to discuss the water, oil, and soap experiment with their families. Suggest that children try variations on these activities at home with their families.

Texture Projector

Standard

Knows that tools can be used to gather information and extend the senses

Overview

Children examine natural objects such as leaves, bark, and twigs and make rubbings with paper and crayons. They use a magnifying glass to examine them more closely.

Materials

- leaves
- twigs
- bark
- crayons with paper removed
- paper
- overhead projector or magnifying glass

Procedure

1. Arrange objects at the center. Invite children to explore the objects, noticing details about how they look, feel, and smell.

2. Demonstrate how to make a rubbing by placing paper over an object and rubbing with a dark crayon. Encourage children to experiment using different colored crayons and to add different objects to their rubbings.

3. When children are finished exploring a few objects, place them on the overhead projector one by one. For space constraints, you may wish to distribute magnifying glasses to children to explore individually. Ask children what they notice about the object when it is magnified.

4. Provide children time to examine the images of the projected objects, and discuss which features appeared in the rubbings that do not appear the same when the objects are magnified.

Texture Projector *(cont.)*

Extension

Provide children with metal objects such as screws, nuts, bolts, and washers to replicate the activity. Ask them to describe how this experience is similar or different from the one using natural objects.

Home Connection

Send home the Family Letter (page 198), suggesting that children bring in natural objects that they find around their homes. Invite families to create rubbings with familiar objects from their homes, and ask children to bring them in to share with the class.

Magic Messages

Standard

Knows that learning can come from careful observations and simple experiments

Overview

Children explore writing letters and images, using lemon juice and water. They will discover what happens when the paper upon which they write is held up to a warm light.

Materials

- lemon juice
- small bowl
- water
- eyedropper
- spoon
- toothpicks or cotton swabs
- white paper
- lamp or sunny window

Procedure

1. Squeeze fresh lemon juice into a small bowl, and ask children to add a few drops of water to the juice, using an eyedropper. Ask another child to mix the water with the spoon.

2. Model how to dip a toothpick or a cotton swab into the mixture, and use it to write or draw on a sheet of white paper. Wait for the mixture to dry so it becomes invisible.

3. Hold the paper close to a warm lamp, a lightbulb, or a warm sunny window to observe the images as they emerge.

4. Invite children to explore the materials and create their own magic messages.

Extension

Experiment with other liquids (e.g., orange juice, milk) to see what happens when they are used to make magic messages. Have children compare them to see how each looks.

Home Connection

Send home the Family Letter (page 198), suggesting that children make magic messages with family members at home. Ask them to share their experiences during a large-group time.

Egg Float

Procedure

1. Gently place an egg in one of the tall glasses of water. Ask children to describe what happens. (The egg should sink to the bottom of the glass.) Have them sketch what the egg looks like in the first glass on the Egg Float Experiment Sheet.

2. Stir several tablespoons of salt into the second tall glass of water, letting children take turns pouring and stirring. Once the water and salt are blended, pour more water into the glass, almost to the top. Do not stir the mixture because you want to make sure the freshwater rests on top of the saltwater.

3. Gently place an egg in the second glass of water (the saltwater) and notice what happens. (The egg should float.) Ask children to describe what happens. Then have them sketch what the egg looks like in the second glass on the Egg Float Experiment Sheet.

4. Discuss with children their hypotheses for why the outcomes were different.

Egg Float (cont.)

Extension

Ask children to survey the other children, asking them for their predictions about whether the eggs will sink or float. Children can compile a graph to display the results, and the class may explore the reasons behind their guesses during a large-group time.

Home Connection

Send home the Family Letter (page 198), suggesting that children try this experiment with their families, using raw eggs and hardboiled eggs. Ask them to compare their results and share the results with the class.

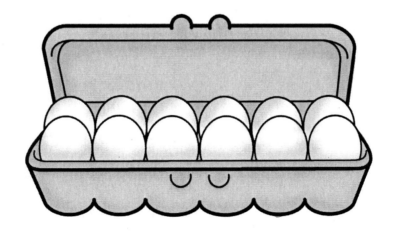

Egg Float Experiment Sheet

Name: _____ Date: _____

Directions: Draw the position of the egg in the water without salt.

Directions: Draw the position of the egg in the water with salt.

#51019—Successful Centers

Weather Wheels

Procedure

1. Discuss the various materials at the center and their purposes with children. Explain that they will use these materials to create a Weather Wheel.

2. Discuss common types of weather with children, such as sunny, cloudy, rainy, snowy, and windy. Invite children to decorate their Weather Wheels with four different pictures, depicting four different kinds of weather.

3. Attach paper arrows to the plates, using the metal brads, and ask children to adjust their arrows to depict the current weather. Children may choose to look out of a classroom window to make their informed decisions, describing the weather using descriptive language. Weather Wheels can be hung near windows around the room so that children can make adjustments throughout the day.

Standard

Knows that short-term weather conditions can change daily, and weather patterns can change over seasons

Overview

Children learn about their local weather and represent the weather conditions with Weather Wheels.

Materials

- paper plates
- metal brads/brass fasteners
- small cardboard or construction paper
- crayons
- markers
- string

Preparation Notes

- Divide paper plates into quarters with a black marker.
- Cut cardboard or construction paper into small arrow shapes (one for each child).

Weather Wheels (cont.)

Extension

Acquire and present some nonfiction books about weather as well as some weather-themed children's books. Children can also explore weather-related sites on the classroom computer to learn about local weather, weather patterns, and weather around the world.

Home Connection

Send home the Family Letter (page 198), inviting children to use their Weather Wheels to track weather over time. Children can share with the class the different types of weather they experienced with their families.

© Shell Education

Shadow Sketches

Procedure

1. Instruct children to explore the shadows of various objects by placing them on a windowsill or an overhead projector. Discuss with them the elements of light and dark and of silhouette and outline.

2. Suggest that children experiment with their own shadows, working with a partner by tracing the outlines of their shadows while standing against a piece of paper taped to the wall. Alternatively, paper may be placed on the ground to capture a shadow cast on the ground. Children can experiment to find the best placement for the paper.

3. Ask children to predict changes in shadows when the light sources are closer and farther from the object. Trace outlines closer and farther from the light source. Discuss what children observe, and consider reasons why the shadows change depending on the proximity and angle of the light source.

Shadow Sketches (cont.)

Extension

Tape a piece of paper to a wall that receives direct sunlight. Place an object on the windowsill, or tape an object to the window. Children record what the shadow looks like at hourly intervals, tracing the outline of the object as the sunlight changes over the course of a day.

Home Connection

Send home the Family Letter (page 198), encouraging children and families to notice their shadows while inside and outside their homes. Children can share their experiences and stories with the class during group time or a small-group activity.

Find the Baby

Standard

Knows that learning can come from careful observations and simple experiments

Overview

Children examine pictures of children at different ages and try to match the baby picture with a current picture of each child.

Materials

- photos of each child as a baby and at his or her current age.

Preparation Notes

- Ask families to send in baby photos of their children.

- Take current photos of each child to use as a comparison.

- You may wish to create an answer key for children to reference after they make their guesses.

Procedure

1. Display baby photos and current photos at the center. Allow time for children to silently examine the photos.

2. Select one baby picture, and ask children to notice features of that child, such as eye color, hair color, qualities of a smile, facial features (e.g., dimples, chin structure), and so on. When many different features have been noted, ask children to work together to guess whose picture it is. If children answer correctly, remove the two photos from the table and set them aside.

3. Continue with the game, alternating with a baby photo as the starting point and the current photo as the starting point, each time noticing features that may be consistent over several years of life as well as features that have changed over time.

Find the Baby (cont.)

Extension

Create a list of observed ways the children have grown and changed. Have children create Venn diagrams with their respective photographs, examining the concepts of *now* and *then*. Children can determine things that they could not do when they were younger and smaller, compared to what they can do now. Invite children to write or draw about favorite memories from earlier childhood.

Home Connection

Send home the Family Letter (page 198), asking families to send in photographs of family members at different ages. Match the pictures based on features. Children may wish to examine photographs of favorite pets taken at two different times of life.

Nature Mural

Standard

Uses the senses to make observations about living things, nonliving objects, and events

Overview

Children take a short nature walk around the school, gathering small objects that they find along the way. Objects are examined and used to contribute to a nature mural.

Materials

- paper (large enough to cover one wall)
- paint
- paintbrushes
- tape
- glue

Preparation Note

Invite an adult volunteer to assist with the nature walk. You may wish to have the whole class go together or have the adult volunteer take the center group.

Procedure

1. Take children on a short nature walk around the school, looking carefully at nature as they walk. You may wish to have an adult volunteer help with this. Invite children to notice grass, flowers, trees, rocks, animals, bugs, and other natural elements.

2. Instruct children to pick up one or two objects of interest to bring back to the classroom. Suggest that leaves and flowers on the ground are preferred to ones that are still attached to their plants, trees, or roots. Discuss this strategy, generating ideas about responsibility for living things and the environment.

3. Once back in the classroom, arrange all of the items children collected at the center, examining each one as a group, and noting their features.

4. Invite children to paint a nature mural during center time that may include natural elements that they saw on the nature walk as well as items that they know from books and their own imaginations. Children may choose to include their nature walk items on the mural also, using glue or tape as needed.

Nature Mural *(cont.)*

Extension

Create a specific theme for a nature mural, such as a jungle mural, an ocean mural, a forest mural, or a tundra mural. Provide children with books related to the environments being explored and discussed, and investigate online resources that may engage children in relevant interactive learning opportunities.

Home Connection

Send home the Family Letter (page 198), inviting family members into the classroom to share their knowledge about nature. For example, one parent may share his or her love of gardening, and another parent may share his or her artifacts from when he or she lived in Alaska.

Listening Jars

Standard

Uses the senses to make observations about living things, nonliving objects, and events

Overview

Children examine Listening Jars, describe the sounds they hear, and try to find two jars that have matching sounds.

Materials

- empty baby food jars (10)

- small objects (e.g., paper clips, rice, metal nuts and bolts)

- black paint or construction paper.

Preparation Note

- Fill every two jars with the same types of objects so that each jar will have a matching jar sound.

- Paint the baby food jars so that the items inside the jars cannot be seen. You may wish to cover the jars with construction paper instead.

Procedure

1. Present the jars to children at the center. Shake a few jars, and have children observe the sound each makes. Explain that there is another jar that will have the same sound.

2. Have children work with the center group to shake, listen, and find the jars with the matching sounds.

3. As children find matches among the jars, ask them to describe the similarities and differences among the sounds.

4. Have children open the paired up jars to see if they have matched them correctly. Ask them to discuss the results with the group.

Listening Jars *(cont.)*

Extension

Children can explore materials using other senses such as touch and smell, using baby food jars with holes in the lid (smell) and paper bags (touch). For example, place small items with different scents (e.g., cinnamon sticks, black peppercorns, chocolate chips) in the jars and ask children to try to find pairs of jars with matching smells. **Note:** Please be aware of food allergies children may have prior to implementing this activity.

Home Connection

Send home the Family Letter (page 198) asking children to explore their homes using their senses. Explain that children will use their hearing, sight, touch, and smell to make simple observations at home. Have children draw pictures of objects they sensed.

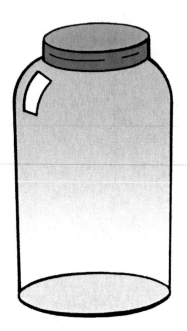

Balancing Act

Standard

Knows that learning can come from careful observations and simple experiments

Overview

Children experiment with various weights by placing objects on a string.

Materials

- string or yarn
- cardboard or heavy cardstock cutouts (e.g., people, animals)
- stickers
- play dough (store-bought or from recipe on page 100)

Preparation Note

Create a "tightrope" for children by tying string to two chairs.

Procedure

1. Show children the tightrope. Model how to place a cutout on the string and to adjust the cutout to try to balance it. Explain that the weight of the cutout must be even on all sides of the string to be able to balance.

2. Ask children to experiment using different cutouts in different ways. For example, a tall, thin shape may balance in a different manner from that of a wider, asymmetrical shape. Discuss the concept of a *center of gravity*.

3. Suggest that children try adding weight to parts of the figures to distribute weight evenly. Children may choose to add stickers to one shape, or stick small pieces of play dough to parts of a figure. Ask them to share their hypotheses and strategies as they experiment.

Extension

Invite children to notice the actions that lead to successful balancing and to create visual/written instructions that can be used in a How-to Book for children who are new to this activity.

Home Connection

Send home the Family Letter (page 198), inviting children to practice balancing small objects at home with their families. For example, they can explore balancing a spoon on their noses or balancing a plastic straw on a drinking cup.

Play Dough Recipe

Ingredients:

- $1\frac{1}{2}$ C water
- 3 C flour
- $\frac{1}{2}$ C salt
- $\frac{1}{4}$ C oil
- Food coloring

Directions:

1. In a large bowl, mix together ingredients.

2. Knead dough with hands to reach desired consistency.

3. Divide dough into portions. You may wish to use food coloring during this activity to achieve desired colors.

Note: Be aware of children's allergies prior to having them work with the play dough.

Social Studies Centers

We shape clay into a pot, but it is the emptiness inside that holds whatever we want.

—Lao Tzu, *Tao Te Ching*

Social Studies learning centers provide opportunities for teachers and children to foster relationships within the school, community, and family members and integrate these with developmentally appropriate, engaging curriculum. Through hands-on experiences that appeal to children's physical, cognitive, and social-emotional inquiry, children learn to appreciate and celebrate diversity as well as the common bonds between and within humanity and nature. Teachers can expand the boundaries of the classroom to include the neighborhood as well as local and distant cultures and traditions through field trips and classroom visits with special guests. The 10 centers in this section connect children with the past, present, and their own future in an ever-changing society. Such experiences bring about a greater understanding of the world and the children's own impact on the broader community.

Calendar Collage

Standard

Knows the holidays and ceremonies of different societies

Overview

Children create collages using various materials to represent dates on a calendar.

Materials

- Calendar Book (pages 104–116)
- photographs, magazines, and newspapers
- glue
- scissors
- glue
- markers

Preparation Note

Inform parents of this activity a week or two in advance, and invite them to contribute magazines for the class project as well as any relevant items for their children to use in their individual calendars (e.g., ticket stubs, photographs, wrappers/labels).

Procedure

1. Discuss various types of special dates with children, such as birthdays and holidays. Encourage them to provide cultural celebrations they celebrate with their families. Invite children to share what makes these events special.

2. Have children think about the months of the year. Ask them to pick a special event for each month of the year.

3. Provide children with photographs, newspapers, and magazines. Have them cut out pictures that remind them of the special dates they have chosen. Ask them to glue the images on the appropriate pages.

4. Once children are finished, bind their pages in the correct order to create a book. You may wish to have children decorate the cover for their books. Allow time for children to share and describe their books with the members in the center.

Calendar Collage (cont.)

Extension

Have children prepare invitations for their families to come into class to view their calendar books. Mark the date accordingly on the classroom calendar. The class may wish to count down the days until the classroom celebration.

Home Connection

Send home the Family Letter (page 198), inviting children to interview members of their families and/or neighbors and friends to learn about the history behind family traditions. Suggest that children identify and add new special days to the class calendar as the year progresses.

My Calendar Book

By _____

January

February

March

April

May

June

July

August

September

October

November

December

A Room of My Own

Procedure

1. Show children examples of floor plans. Explain that each represents an actual room. Point out the features of each example. You may wish to place floor plans on an overhead projector to magnify the plan's features.

2. Ask children to think about a room for which they would like to create a floor plan. Have them place small objects out in front of them to represent objects in the room they have chosen.

3. Distribute paper to children to draw the layout of the small objects they have placed in front of them. Have them label or dictate what each object represents.

4. Give children time to share and describe their floor plans to the group.

A Room of My Own (cont.)

Extension

Invite children to find items in the classroom that start with different letters of the alphabet and bring them to the rug for a large-group time. One by one, invite children to place items in the center of the rug while the rest of the children close their eyes. Ask children to notice what has been added and what has changed in terms of placement and perspective. You may also wish to read *The Alphabet Room* by Sara Pinto (2003) to children. While reading, point out how the illustrations change as items are added to the room one by one.

Home Connection

Send home the Family Letter (page 198), inviting families to take a photograph of a favorite room in their home or a special room in a different location. Ask families to write a brief description of the room and what makes it so special and send it into the classroom. Children can share their photographs with the class.

Family and Friends Time Lines

Standard

Knows how to develop picture time lines of their own lives or their family's history

Overview

Children create accordion book time lines denoting historical or family events.

Materials

- craft paper on a roll or long strips of paper
- crayons
- markers
- colored pencils

Preparation Note

Create a sample accordion time line in advance with specific events that have occurred sequentially for each square on the accordion.

Procedure

1. Share the sample time line you created with students, emphasizing words such as *before*, *after*, and *next*. Explain that a time line is a way to show the order in which events have taken place.

2. Tell children that they will create their own time lines. Ask them what they like to do with family and friends on special occasions, holidays, or other important dates.

3. Have children dictate or write one specific date per square on the accordion and then illustrate the specific events over time.

4. When children have finished their time lines, set up a display together so that children may explore one another's time lines and ask one another questions about the events.

Family and Friends Time Lines (cont.)

Extension

Suggest that children create time lines for a favorite pet, hero, or imaginary character. They may wish to work in pairs to represent activities shared with a friend.

Home Connection

Send home the Family Letter (page 198), inviting families to visit the class to describe one or two events on their child's time line. They may wish to bring in artifacts or important memorabilia that represent the specific event.

Photo Diaries

Standard

Knows how to develop picture time lines of their own lives or their family's history

Overview

Children take photos of activities during the course of one day or weekend and organize the photos in a sequence.

Materials

- camera
- computer and printer
- photos (5 per child)
- construction paper
- markers

Preparation Note

A week in advance, inform families of the Photo Diaries activity and get a sense of which families do or do not have access to a camera. If a classroom camera is available to share, families may take turns using the camera for one day at a time, respectively, over the course of a week or two. (**Option:** Families can utilize cell phones with cameras and send their photos in via email).

Procedure

1. Ask children to share the photos they have collected with the center group, placing them in chronological order and briefly explaining/describing the photos.

2. Distribute construction paper to children. Model how to glue the photos in the order in which they occurred to create their books.

3. Have children place their photos on the pages and create books that depict a day in their lives or a weekend. Children may dictate or write one or two sentence captions for each photo.

Photo Diaries *(cont.)*

Extension

When children complete their diaries, they may wish to add them to the classroom library so that classmates can explore them. Ask children to dictate or write comments for the authors/creators and invite children to respond to these questions during a whole-group time.

Home Connection

Send home the Family Letter (page 198), inviting families into the classroom for a "gallery walk" to explore the photo diaries. This can be accompanied by a celebratory breakfast or other reception, featuring favorite family treats.

Time Capsule

Standard

Knows ways in which people share family beliefs and values

Overview

Children create a classroom time capsule that will be stored by the teacher and opened at a future date.

Materials

- waterproof and/or airtight box (one per center group)
- construction paper
- markers
- magazines
- glue
- index cards
- pencils and pens
- newspaper
- other items to be determined by the group

Procedure

1. Discuss the notion of a time capsule with the center group. Invite children to share ideas about why people create time capsules and what they would want to put inside for a class time capsule such as their school name and symbol or their families' beliefs and traditions.

2. Brainstorm ideas about what items the children want to place in their class time capsule, what the best containers are for long-term storage, and who the audience is for their time capsule.

3. Invite children to decorate the container with construction paper and markers and/or collage with images from magazines.

4. During the course of the week, while children are in the process of decorating the container, invite them to also draw pictures and dictate or write letters on index cards to the future viewers of the time capsule contents. Children may choose to include a current newspaper and small items such as artworks, photographs, and other materials (with caregivers' permission).

5. Have children place the contents in the time capsule container and seal it. Culminate the activity with a celebratory snack or photograph to commemorate the event.

Time Capsule *(cont.)*

Extension

Read the picture book *Flotsam* by David Wiesner (2006) during whole-group time. Discuss the way that the protagonist in this story communicates with others over time. Brainstorm other ways that people may communicate with one another over time and distances.

Home Connection

Send home the Family Letter (page 198), inviting families to contribute a letter to the classroom time capsule. Families may also be encouraged to share current newspapers, magazines, ticket stubs from local transportation, or receipts that indicate costs of items.

Community Workers

Procedure

1. Show children pictures of people who work in the community. Discuss each picture while asking children about the jobs shown in each one and why we need them in the community.

2. Have children think about an admirable person who works in their community. Ask them to explain why they have chosen the person.

3. Once children have identified a particular individual whom they admire or find interesting, provide them with a person template to decorate. You may wish to describe the uniforms of the chosen community workers to children.

4. Children may dictate or write a few sentences on a separate sheet of paper that represent the person. Arrange the people and captions on a wall in the classroom so that the class has an opportunity to "meet" a range of people who have made a difference in the community.

Community Workers (cont.)

Extension

Take a field trip to a local museum and note examples of bravery evident in artwork, inventions, or other artifacts. Ask a docent or other volunteer to share information about the impact of specific works on society. You may also wish to have clothes that represent community workers for children to use for role-play.

Home Connection

Send home the Family Letter (page 198), encouraging children and families to read a biography of a person of interest at home. Children can share their new knowledge and stories with the class.

Person Template

Name: _____ **Date:** _____

Directions: Draw a uniform or symbols to represent the community worker you admire.

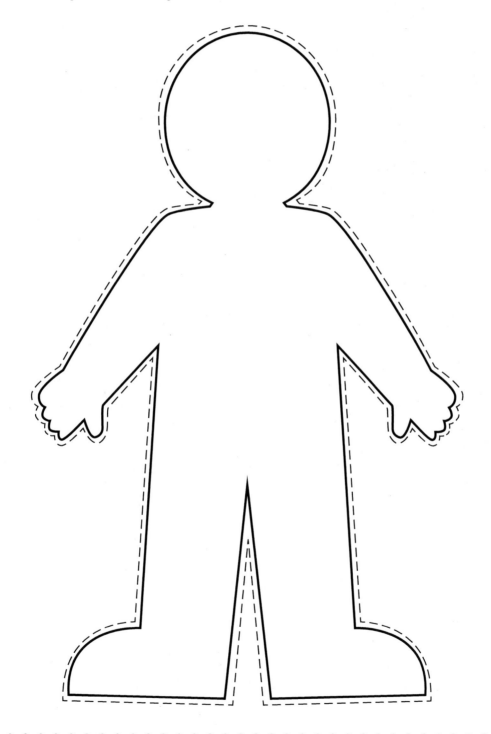

Exercise Your Rights

Standard

Understands rules and the purposes they serve

Overview

Children conduct a survey to learn about different options for exercise.

Materials

- Exercise Graph (page 129)
- pencils
- computer and/or local newspapers

Procedure

1. Talk with children about the health benefits of play and exercise. Discuss opportunities for children and families to play outdoors and exercise in the community. Create a list of the suggestions. Talk about the rules that each activity has in place so that people can play or exercise together fairly.

2. Show children the Exercise Graph sheet. Ask them to choose four exercises for the graph to be based on. Have them ask fellow classmates about their favorite one out of the four. Model how to mark a person's choice on the graph.

3. Once they have gathered the data, examine and discuss the results of the graph with the group, noting patterns and unusual findings.

Extension

Invite children to share their findings with a local legislator. Children may have specific requests for funding that could enhance neighborhood play spaces and recreation. Invite the legislator to speak with children about local commitments to citizens' health and fitness.

Home Connection

Send home the Family Letter (page 198), inviting children to survey family members about their favorite forms of outdoor activity/exercise. Combine children's results on a classroom graph and share the results in a family newsletter. You may wish to have families suggest classroom activities or outings for the class to do.

Exercise Graph

10+			
9			
8			
7			
6			
5			
4			
3			
2			
1			

_____ _____ _____ _____

My School

Standard

Understands that maps can represent his or her surroundings

Overview

Children observe individuals and buildings as they walk around the school.

Materials

- map of the school
- camera(s)
- pencils
- paper
- tape
- glue
- paint
- paintbrushes

Preparation Note

You may wish to take the entire class on the walk or have an adult volunteer take the center group.

Procedure

1. Show children a map of the school. Point out features on the map that children are familiar with, such as the lunch area and the bathrooms. Take the group on a walk around the school, looking carefully as they walk and noting the different features that were on the map. Have children notice and record who and what they see with cameras or pencils and paper.

2. Invite children to generate or dictate a list of characteristics that describe the school environment.

3. Once back in the classroom, discuss the features that children remember.

4. Invite children to create a mural of the school, which may include photographs of people/places that they saw on their walk(s) as well as things that they know from their own experiences.

My School *(cont.)*

Extension

Choose one particular store or business to get to know well. Visit the store several times, becoming familiar with employees and products. Children may draw or write about the store. Their work may be displayed in the store for community members to appreciate. Share the relationship with a local newspaper to publicize the relationship and the impact that the experience has had on children and families.

Home Connection

Send home the Family Letter (page 198), inviting family members into the classroom to share their knowledge about a neighborhood resource. For example, one parent may discuss his or her work, and another parent may share artifacts that represent the impact of that resource on the broader community.

Where Would I Build a Home?

Standard

Understands the globe as a representation of the Earth

Overview

Children examine a globe to become familiar with different parts that represent Earth.

Materials

- globe
- map
- computer
- children's atlases

Procedure

1. Place the globe at the center and invite children to explore it. Have them discuss the various colors and what they represent (blue = water, green/brown = land, white = ice). Explain that the globe represents the planet we live on, Earth. Point out the region in which the school is located.

2. Invite children to choose and focus on a particular place or region that they would like to live. Examine this place on a map, an atlas, or a computer, and compare how Earth looks against what it looks like on the globe, noting differences in representation and/or appearance (e.g., bumpy on the globe; smooth on the map).

3. Ask children to think about the weather, based on location, and to note the distance between their home and the specific location. Discuss different ways children would travel to this location, what they would need to pack, and other details.

Where Would I Build a Home? *(cont.)*

Extension

Have children learn more about their chosen destination or region. Travel agencies may provide materials such as maps and brochures that describe the location in more detail.

 ## Home Connection

Send home the Family Letter (page 198), inviting family members to share specific travel experiences with the class, including photos, souvenirs, and other items. Guest visitors may choose to present their destinations in a mystery format, where children guess the location based on clues the family members provide.

Classroom Bank

Standard

Knows that a price is the amount of money that people pay when they buy a good or service

Overview

Children become familiar with the role of banks in the lives of citizens.

Materials

various bank items (e.g., deposit and/or withdrawal slips, calculators, paper coin rolls, play money)

Preparation Notes

As a class, take a field trip to a local bank, or invite a bank employee to visit the classroom. Ask them to describe a typical bank visit, such as making a withdrawal. Make a list of specific vocabulary used, such as *deposit* and *checkbook*.

Procedure

1. Discuss the role that banks play. Give children time to share experiences they have had with banks. Explain that people often go to banks to take out money to buy things such as a good (a book) or a service (a car wash).

2. Distribute various bank materials at the center. Invite children to explore the materials and to think about how they are used at the bank. Have them work with the group to create their own bank scenarios in the dramatic play area.

3. Encourage children to compose a letter to the bank staff, thanking them for the recent visit. Include photographs and/or drawings that illustrate the children's new understandings of banking and the role of banks in the community.

Classroom Bank *(cont.)*

Extension

Have children work with partners and explore play money. Distribute various coins and bills for children to play with and compare. One of the partners can ask for a specific amount of money while the other partner counts it out to them. Then, partners can switch roles.

Home Connection

Send home the Family Letter (page 198), asking families to donate pennies, old checks or checkbooks, and other items relating to money, banks, and the broader financial world for children to include in dramatic play.

Art Centers

Singing has always seemed to me the most perfect means of expression. It is so spontaneous. And after singing, I think the violin. Since I cannot sing, I paint.

—Georgia O'Keeffe (1887–1986)

Art learning centers are unique by their very nature, with an emphasis on the creative process and creative expression rather than completed products. Children should be encouraged to explore materials and to take healthy risks with their ideas. Experimenting with different materials is emphasized, conveying to children that they are respected and that teachers and children are experts in executing their respective ideas. Art Center activities include visual arts such as drawing and painting as well as expressive arts such as movement, dance, and drama. Because creativity has no boundaries, varied opportunities to engage in art activities should be presented, and teachers must learn to be comfortable with some degree of mess and different energy from what is typically required in table activities. Establishing routines for Art Center activities is important so that children take responsibility for the area, the materials, themselves, and each other.

Color Dance

Standard

Experiments with a variety of color, textures, and shapes

Overview

Children explore the ways colors "dance" on the surface of liquid and how they can manipulate the colors and movement with simple tools.

Materials

- pie tin or shallow baking dish
- whole milk
- small bowls
- dish soap
- food coloring or liquid watercolors
- eyedroppers
- cotton swabs
- toothpicks
- camera

Preparation Note

- Pour milk in the pie tin so that there is a thick layer of milk covering the bottom, and leave it at the center.
- Pour some dish soap in small bowls, and leave them at the center.

Procedure

1. Invite children to drop food coloring into the milk and watch what happens. Encourage children to describe the effects of the colors on the white surface of the milk.

2. Provide children with toothpicks and cotton swabs. Instruct them to dip the end of a toothpick or cotton swab into a bowl with the dish soap. Then have them dip the toothpick into a colored area of milk in the pie tin.

3. Ask children to describe how the colors "dance" on the surface of the milk, using descriptive language to prompt their vocabulary. Take photos of the color dancing to use at a subsequent Art Center or large-group discussion in order to revisit learning and understanding about colors, movement, and cause and effect.

Color Dance *(cont.)*

Extension

Children may experiment with color mixing before and after adding the dish soap, making predictions about which colors will blend and which colors will retain their properties when added to the milk together. Children can attempt to gently place a white sheet of paper on the surface of the liquid to see if the Color Dance creates a print. Different textures and thicknesses of paper may yield different results.

Home Connection

Send home the Family Letter (page 198), asking families to repeat the experiment at home. Ask families to share their experiences and any suggestions for future Color Dances.

Mirror Me

Standard

Moves his or her body in a variety of controlled ways

Overview

Children use mirrors to re-create and invent movements and expressions.

Materials

- 1 or 2 full-length mirrors
- Movement Cards (pages 140–141)

Preparation Note

You may wish to laminate the Movement Cards for durability.

Procedure

1. Provide children with an assortment of cards. Each card depicts some form of movement or expression. Children close their eyes and choose one card to examine closely.

2. Standing in front of a full-length mirror, each child practices copying the movement and/or expressions depicted on his or her card.

3. When children have each had turns re-creating movements using the laminated cards, instruct them to form a circle, facing each other.

4. Children will take turns creating their own movements as the rest of the group watches closely to notice precise gestures and facial expressions. Children may volunteer individually or with peers to imitate or "mirror" the new movement.

Extension

Children can be challenged to create movements to respond to different kinds of music. Children will move quickly, slowly, in small ways, and in large ways according to how they perceive the music.

Home Connection

Send home the Family Letter (page 198), inviting families to share favorite dance movements and music from their homes and/or cultural traditions. You may wish to ask them to come in and show the class.

Movement Cards

Craft Stick Puppets

Standard

Creates props to support dramatic play

Overview

Children make puppets with various materials, design background images, and create stories to share with others.

Materials

- large craft sticks
- colored markers
- glue
- small decorative items (e.g., buttons, sequins, ribbon, yarn, beads)
- paper
- shoe boxes
- scissors

Procedure

1. Inform children that they will tell stories to each other using craft stick puppets that they will create. Brainstorm some ideas for stories and characters that they would like to create. You may wish to have children work independently or with peers.

2. Invite children to use the various items to decorate their Craft Stick Puppets. Provide children with feedback as needed to enhance the puppet creations or extend their thinking.

3. While the Craft Stick Puppets are drying, children may decorate the setting/scenery for their puppet shows. They may choose paper or a shoe box and use colored markers and other materials to create the desired scenes.

4. Ask children to point to places in the scenery where they would like the puppets to appear, poking their heads out of the paper/shoe box. Use scissors to cut slits large enough for the Craft Stick Puppets to emerge, and invite children to enjoy practicing and performing their puppet-theater productions.

Extension

Challenge children to create stories around a specific theme that ties in to other content-area curriculum or themes. For example, they may create a story about a science experiment for a science connection or about someone working at his or her job for a social studies connection.

 ## Home Connection

Send home the Family Letter (page 198), inviting children to bring their puppets with them on vacations or weekend visits. Have them write or draw about their puppet adventures to share with the class.

My City, Your City

Standard

Experiments with a variety of color, textures, and shapes

Overview

Children consider how to make two-dimensional designs to represent a city.

Materials

- recyclable materials (e.g., milk cartons, newspaper, toilet paper/paper-towel tubes)
- wood pieces
- chenille sticks
- packing peanuts
- glue
- paint
- paintbrushes
- colored markers
- paper
- pencils

Preparation Note

Ask families to donate recyclable materials for children to use at the center.

Procedure

1. Invite children to imagine a new city that they will design and create using a variety of materials. Discuss what cities look like and some characteristics of cities, such as buildings, streets, stores, cars, and people.

2. Introduce the bounty of items to children. Older children may wish to sketch their city plans using pencils and paper while thinking about which items they will use to turn their ideas into actual constructions. Younger children may want to dive right in.

3. Have children start building their cities, adding items to the larger city area (limited only by space available in the Art Center). You may wish to have children work independently or with peers. Once children have built their cities, they can then decorate the cities with paint and other materials.

4. Ask children to look at the city from different perspectives, giving one another suggestions for ways to enhance or improve upon the construction.

My City, Your City (cont.)

Extension

Connect the city building to other content areas, such as reading and writing (e.g., provide fiction and nonfiction books about cities) and math (e.g., use blocks to construct towers and patterns).

Home Connection

Send home the Family Letter (page 198), inviting families to an Open House to explore the new city. During the Open House, have children describe their cities to their families.

Color My Mood

Standard

Uses visual structures and functions to communicate ideas

Overview

Children create artworks to reflect their emotions.

Materials

- examples of artwork
- paper
- paint
- paintbrushes
- colored markers
- crayons

Preparation Note

- Gather examples of artwork.

Procedure

1. Introduce the idea that different colors make us think of different feelings. Show some examples of famous artwork, such as O'Keeffe's *Red Poppy* and Van Gogh's *Sunflowers* compared with Picasso's *The Old Guitarist*, and ask children to describe the mood they believe the artist was feeling and/or trying to convey.

2. Invite children to explore the paints and to create their own mood art. Reassure them that they can paint with whatever colors they want to use. However, if they want to paint a picture that evokes a specific mood, certain colors will best lend themselves to that effort.

Extension

Experiment with different kinds of music that evoke various moods. Play music as children paint their pictures, offering a variety of colors to accompany the music. Invite children to share their artwork and their thoughts during their painting process.

Home Connection

Send home the Family Letter (page 198), encouraging families to discuss different feelings with their children. Suggest that artwork is one way to start conversations with children about how they are feeling.

Let's Take a Line Walk

Standard

Knows the similarities and differences in the meanings of common terms used in various arts

Overview

Children notice how lines connect in our view of the world to form images and designs.

Materials

- camera (optional)
- small notepads
- pencils

Preparation Note

Invite an adult volunteer to assist with the nature walk. You may wish to have the whole class go together or have the adult volunteer take the center group.

Procedure

1. Take children on a "Line Walk" to observe different kinds of lines in the environment. You may wish to have an adult volunteer help with this.

2. As children notice lines, take pictures to revisit later, back in the classroom, and encourage children to stop and copy lines onto their notepads. Suggest that children notice lines that occur in nature (e.g., tree bark, leaves, clouds) and lines that occur in manmade constructions (e.g., fences, walls, windows).

3. Back in the classroom, share images that children sketched on the Line Walk, and supplement them with images from architectural and environmental publications.

4. Have children draw and decorate a picture to represent the object that has a particular line.

5. Ask children for words to describe the different kinds of lines that they observed before offering standard labels (e.g., *jagged*, *straight*, *curved*, *thick*, *thin*). Compare some of the labels, asking them to explain which feels most accurate to describe a specific kind of line.

Let's Take a Line Walk *(cont.)*

Extension

Share with children the book *The Dot and the Line* by Norman Juster (2000). There is also an animated film version. Provide children with circle stamps and thin markers to play with their imagination, making dot-and-line creations.

Home Connection

Send home the Family Letter (page 198), inviting families to create new artwork using various lines discussed in class (e.g., curvy, zigzag, straight) with their children. Have children bring in their designs to share them with the class.

Texture Pizza

Standard

Experiments with a variety of color, textures, and shapes

Overview

Children make collages using materials of various textures to make "pizzas." They recognize that different "slices" can have different textures and appearance.

Materials

- cardboard circles or thick paper plates

- glue

- materials of various textures (e.g., pieces of sandpaper, fake fur, velvet, Mylar, hard plastic, cotton balls)

- yarn (cut the length of the diameter of the circles or paper plates)

Preparation Note

Place various materials at the center. Show children the materials and discuss the different textures they have.

Procedure

1. Ask children to share what they know about pizza, such as what a pizza looks like and how it is divided into slices.

2. Ask children to think about how they will make their Texture Pizza. For example, they might begin by selecting their "ingredients" and getting them ready to use. Next, they might spread or drizzle glue as the "sauce" that they spread on their circles and then add their ingredients.

3. Children can place their pizzas on a rack to dry (or "cook") and then glue yarn in a crisscross pattern to divide the pizza into slices, or have a teacher cut the circle into the desired number of slices.

Texture Pizza *(cont.)*

Extension

Ask children to describe why they chose particular "ingredients" for their Texture Pizzas, noting the features of the specific items. The pizzas can also be used in dramatic play or math activities.

Home Connection

Send home the Family Letter (page 198), inviting families to share their favorite kinds of pizza or pizza recipes. Compile a class pizza book that features photos of children and families eating pizza alongside the recipes.

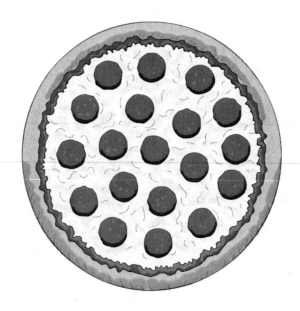

Blot a Lot

Standard

Experiments with a variety of color, textures, and shapes

Overview

Children create inkblot paintings using paints and folding paper.

Materials

- large sheets of paper
- tempera or poster paint
- colored markers

Preparation Note

Create a few inkblot paintings to provide children with examples.

Procedure

1. Model for children how to fold their sheets of paper in half.

2. Instruct children to open their creased papers, and to choose a color of paint to use. Invite them to drop a spoonful of paint into the middle of their creased paper, and to refold the paper along the crease.

3. Show children how they will next press the folded paper, noticing the feeling of the paint between the halves of paper. Ask children to describe how the paint feels between the halves of paper.

4. Invite children to open their papers, revealing their inkblot paintings. Point out how the images are symmetrical (same on both sides of the page). Ask them to describe what their paintings look like. After paintings have dried, children may choose to add details to their creations with paint and/or colored markers or to leave them as they are.

Blot a Lot *(cont.)*

Extension

Print out examples of inkblots and take turns choosing one to describe. Children may wish to combine their inkblot paintings into a larger creation. Read the children's book *It Looked Like Spilt Milk* (1993) by Charles G. Shaw. Together, notice the images in that book and discuss what makes those shapes different from the symmetrical ones created in the inkblot activity.

Home Connection

Send home the Family Letter (page 198), suggesting that parents find opportunities to explore symmetry in their homes, such as in furniture, carpet designs, sheets and bedding, and ceiling patterns.

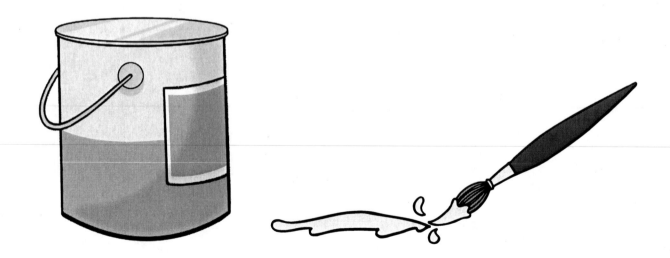

Scrappy Books

Standard

Uses visual structures and functions to communicate ideas

Overview

Children create a book out of recycled materials and learn about recycling and conservation.

Materials

- scraps of paper
- construction paper
- glue
- string or yarn

Preparation Note

Begin gathering scraps of paper in a designated box to use for this center activity. You may wish to bring in magazines and newspapers as well.

Procedure

1. Explain to children that they will use scrap paper to create artwork. Show examples of famous artwork using collage, such as works by Pablo Picasso and Max Ernst. Discuss what is interesting about their artwork and how they might have used paper and glue to create them.

2. Place the scrap box in the middle of the table. Provide each child with a sheet of construction paper to use as the cover for his or her Scrappy Book. Have them fold it to make the cover. Tell them to use the scraps of paper that they can cut, rip, weave, twist, and glue accordingly to decorate their covers.

3. Once children are finished, staple blank sheets of paper inside for them to write in or to create drawings in.

Extension

Have children use the book for other subject areas. They may use the books to write or draw notes during a lesson or keep it as a daily journal.

 ## Home Connection

Send home the Family Letter (page 198), inviting families to send in interesting scraps of paper from wrapping paper, old calendars, and other sources.

What Would Happen If...?

Standard

Experiments with a variety of color, textures, and shapes

Overview

Children take turns recording the outcomes of color experiments, making predictions about changes that will or will not occur.

Materials

- tempera or poster paints
- watercolors in primary colors
- oil pastels
- crayons
- paper

Procedure

1. Tell children that they will be art scientists and that they will experiment using different colors of paint and other materials to answer the question *What would happen if...?*

2. Begin by modeling for children how they can combine primary colors to discover secondary colors on paper. For example, demonstrate what happens when red is mixed with yellow. Ask children to describe what happens when the two colors are mixed together.

3. Suggest that children conduct their own experiment using red and blue. Discuss the outcomes as a group.

4. Invite children to try mixing colors together, blending watercolors with tempera paint. Do they get the same result as when using two colors of the same kind of paint? What happens if they try mixing colors using pastels or crayons? What other combinations might they explore?

What Would Happen If...? *(cont.)*

Extension

Record the outcomes from this activity on a chart. Share the chart during whole-group time, and ask children to generate hypotheses about why colors change into new colors when they are mixed together. You may wish to make this activity available at the Art Center and the Science Center if interest and motivation are high.

Home Connection

Send home the Family Letter (page 198), inviting families to read *Little Blue and Little Yellow* (1995) by Leo Lionni together. Encourage them to experiment with colors at home.

Music Centers

Music in the soul can be heard by the universe.

—Lao Tzu

Music learning centers build upon children's natural joy that is evident as they respond to sounds and rhythms. Children learn to appreciate music as a complex form of art and communication. Store-bought and child-created instruments may be found in the Music Center, along with CDs featuring a wide range of music—instrumental and vocal, professionally recorded, and student recorded. The wide variety of materials available for use in the Music Center ensures that children's interest and motivation levels remain consistently strong. Music Centers offer children benefits such as increased opportunities to develop strengths and self-confidence, which are often limited by the demands of a highly structured, teacher-directed curriculum. The activities presented in the Music Center provide children with opportunities to experiment with sounds, musical instruments, and their own compositions while making connections to concepts relating to math, art, language and literacy, culture, and traditions.

Shake It Up

Standard

Echoes short rhythms and melodic patterns

Overview

Children use ordinary household items to create unique musical instruments.

Materials

Possible materials include:

- boxes of different sizes

- spoons (metal and plastic)

- empty aluminum cans

- pie tins

- plastic cups of different sizes

- toilet paper and paper-towel tubes

- plastic combs

- tape (masking and duct)

- contact paper

- small items (e.g., shells, pennies, buttons, pebbles, paper clips)

- stickers

- colored markers

- string or yarn

Procedure

1. Present children with a wide variety of materials to explore and consider using to create their own instruments. Encourage children to explore the sounds that they can make using various items and combinations of items.

2. Help children, as needed, to cover the openings of boxes and containers and invite them to experiment with the different sounds that different quantities create and that are promoted with different amounts of air flow.

3. When children have finished making their instruments, invite them to decorate the instruments using stickers, colored markers, and yarn.

4. When instruments are finished, create a rhythm for children to repeat, using their instruments.

Shake It Up *(cont.)*

Extension

Children can work together in pairs and small groups to play music in a band. Discuss characteristics band members have, such as respect for one another and dedication.

Home Connection

Send home the Family Letter (page 198), inviting families to visit the class and share their musical talents. Families can also share music and instruments that represent their cultural heritage.

Match My Moves

Standard

Echoes short rhythms and melodic patterns

Overview

Children use instruments to create sounds at specific tempos that match children's movements.

Materials

variety of store-bought and child-made musical instruments

Procedure

1. Invite children to imagine different ways that people move, such as walking, running, crawling, skipping, and twirling.

2. Ask them to think about how their movements change depending on what they are doing and where they are going. For example, on a very hot day, how would they move if they saw lawn sprinklers to cool off in? How would they move if they saw a giant elephant looking at them? How would they move if they just received a giant helium balloon?

3. Ask one child to imagine a way that he or she might move and to demonstrate moving that way within a circular area. Invite another child to choose one of the instruments to accompany his or her movements. The child should use a slow, rhythmic beat or quick tempo accordingly, depending on the moving child's pace, facial expressions, and other gestures. Instruct children to take turns being the child who moves and the child who uses the instrument to match the moves.

Match My Moves *(cont.)*

Extension

Use visualization to imagine sounds that children associate with specific animals and their movements. For example, what would a frog's jumping sound like in a muddy swamp? A rabbit hopping on a gravelly road? A turtle crawling along a wet sidewalk?

Home Connection

Send home the Family Letter (page 198), challenging families to incorporate music and rhythm into their family routines. For example, a parent can suggest that they all walk like turtles to the dinner table or that the grown-ups hop like kangaroos on hot sand and the children glide like snakes down the hallway.

Sentence Sonata

Standard

Echoes short rhythms and melodic patterns

Overview

A child will read, say, or sing one or two sentences while other children use their voices, bodies, and/or musical instruments to mimic the tone and syllable patterns in the sentence(s).

Materials

variety of store-bought and child-made musical instruments

Procedure

1. Have children sit in a circle, and tell them that they will play a music game. Ask them to listen carefully as you say one or two sentences, such as, "I have a pet monkey." Ask children to repeat the sentence(s).

2. Ask another child to "say" the sentence using her voice, body, or musical instrument. For example, the child could clap out, "Clap clap clap clap clap-clap," or shake a shaker, "Shake shake shake shake shake-shake."

3. Suggest a sentence that ends with an exuberant exclamation point, and see how the children choose to imitate the exuberance with their instruments. For example, *I love to swim!* or *Today is my birthday!*

4. Alternatively, offer a sentence that conveys a lazy, slow tone, such as *I feel very sleepy*, or *The snail is moving on the leaf*. Invite children to respond with their instruments.

Extension

Read various poems with children, and invite them to accompany the words with their musical instruments. You may wish to create a class poem together.

Home Connection

Send home the Family Letter (page 198), encouraging families to notice opportunities for making music at home, using instruments or innovative play with household items (e.g., spoons, cups, pots, and pans). Families can create musical "conversations." They will communicate through musical call-and-response—first the child offers music and then the parent responds with music.

Super Sheet Music

Standard

Knows standard symbols used to notate meter, rhythm, pitch, and dynamics in simple patterns

Overview

Children will work together to create a poster-size sheet of music. The teacher will explain the conventions of writing notes and placing them on the lines, and different notes will be played as children represent them.

Materials

- large sheet of poster board or butcher paper
- examples of sheet music
- Super Sheet Music (page 164)
- pencils
- markers
- paint
- paintbrushes

Preparation Notes

- Take a large sheet of poster board or butcher paper and draw lines to create a blank music sheet.
- Draw various symbols for examples to show children.

Procedure

1. Explore some examples of actual sheet music with children. See what children notice.

2. Discuss with children the difference between notes and notations, such as whole notes and quarter notes. Show children the sample you created prior to the center. Briefly explain that different musical notes make different sounds.

3. Place a poster-size sheet of paper and a folder of sheet music in the center for children to examine. Distribute copies of Super Sheet Music, pencils, and markers to each child.

4. Encourage children to work together to make notes on the paper. Suggest that children use pencils on the poster first to decide on placement of notes and then to paint the notes, using colorful paint.

Extension

When children have finished their collaborative sheet music, celebrate with a concert in which children "play" the music. Invite an adult into the classroom to play for and with the children.

 ## Home Connection

Send home the Family Letter (page 198), inviting families to send in old sheet music for children to examine and use for coloring and other art projects.

Super Sheet Music

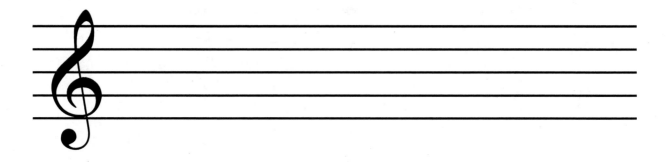

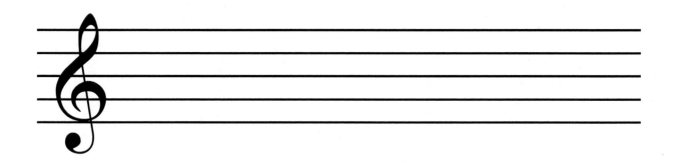

Musical Instrument Medley

Standard

Knows the source of a variety of sounds

Overview

Children use photos and images of musical instruments to create a collage and learn general information about musical sections of an orchestra.

Materials

- variety of photos of musical instruments
- construction paper
- scissors
- glue
- colored markers

Procedure

1. Provide children with a large assortment of pictures of musical instruments. Encourage children to explore the pictures and to identify some of the instruments with which they are familiar.

2. Ask children to sort the instruments into different groups based on characteristics. Explain the traditional groupings of instruments, such as percussion, woodwind, brass, and string instruments.

3. Invite children to create instrument collages with the pictures on construction paper.

Extension

Children can collaborate on a Musical Medley collage, which can serve as the design for a photocopied/scanned invitation that gets sent home to families, inviting them to a class concert.

Home Connection

Send home the Family Letter (page 198), suggesting that families listen to different kinds of music with their children. Encourage them to listen for specific musical instruments within a musical piece and to call attention to them. Invite them to share favorite symphony recordings with the class to listen to during a large-group time.

Dance Around the World

Standard

Knows that music comes from different places and different periods of time

Overview

Children view photographs and video clips of children dancing in different parts of the world and learn one of the dances.

Materials

- different music representing a range of cultural traditions from around the world

Preparation Note

Collect online video clips of children dancing cultural dances to share with children. You may wish to visit **http://www. fitforafeast.com/dance_cultural. htm** for examples.

Procedure

1. Watch video clips of children doing different cultural dances.

2. Discuss what they notice about the dancing and the music. Are there patterns that the children notice? Do the movements match the mood or tempo of the music? Discuss.

3. Teach children a basic dance from a specific culture. Invite children to take turns performing the dances for one another in small groups.

Extension

Discuss traditional costume or dress that accompanies traditional dancing. Invite children to design simple costumes for their dances.

 ## Home Connection

Send home the Family Letter (page 198), inviting children's siblings to class to demonstrate cultural dancing (e.g., Irish Step dance, Salsa, Native American dance, Israeli dance).

Soft Symphony

Standard

Knows the source of a variety of sounds

Overview

Children learn about different tools that musicians use to make their instruments quieter (e.g., brass mute, violin mute), and create their own quiet instruments to play in the class Soft Symphony.

Materials

- paper plates
- cotton balls
- paper cups
- glitter
- glue
- colored markers

Procedure

1. Demonstrate how certain tools can change an instrument's sound, turning a loud sound into a quieter sound. For example, play a violin with and without a violin mute, or show children a video clip featuring someone playing the trumpet with and without a brass mute.

2. Give children an opportunity to experiment with creating sounds with various materials. Explain that they will create musical instruments that will make "soft" sounds and discuss some potential characteristics of soft-sounding instruments.

3. Using the materials provided, invite children to create their instruments. When they have finished creating and decorating their instruments, invite them to play a familiar tune, such as *Old MacDonald Had a Farm*, using their instruments.

Extension

Invite children to create "quiet" dance moves to accompany the Soft Symphony players. Introduce specific music terms, such as *sotto voce*, and how composers specifically choose quieter and louder moments in their compositions.

Home Connection

Send home the Family Letter (page 198), encouraging children to play their soft instruments at home. They can use stuffed animals, pillows, and other "soft" objects to enhance their play.

Musical Jars

Standard

Uses a variety of sound sources when composing

Overview

Children experiment with sounds that are made when glass jars are hit with wooden sticks.

Materials

- identical glass jars (5 or 6)
- water
- wooden sticks (or chopsticks or pencils)

Procedure

1. Arrange the jars in a line on a table. Pour a small amount of water into the first jar, and ask a child to gently hit the side of the jar with a pencil or other wooden stick. Discuss the sound that is made.

2. Pour more water into the next jar, and ask another child to gently hit the side of the jar. Compare the sounds of the two jars, and ask children for their thoughts about how the water levels affect the sounds.

3. Encourage children to experiment by adding water to the jars and listening to the sounds made by striking the jars.

Extension

Create a musical sequence of tones or re-create familiar tunes. Invite children to draw a picture to represent the sequence of jars, or take photos of the jars and discuss during a large-group time.

Home Connection

Send home the Family Letter (page 198), encouraging families to explore this activity at home. Children can teach their families about the different effects to expect using varying levels of water.

Name That Instrument!

Standard

Knows the source of a variety of sounds

Overview

Children work together to explore instruments and then attempt to identify the instruments by sound alone in a game format.

Materials

- various instruments
- screen or other divider to separate children on opposite sides of a table

Procedure

1. Invite children to examine several instruments, using different senses (e.g., listening, looking, and feeling).

2. Move instruments to one side of a screen, and ask one child to sit on the opposite side of the screen.

3. Select another child to choose and play an instrument, making different sounds while the classmate tries to identify the instrument by its sound. Encourage children to take turns playing and guessing the musical instruments.

Extension

To simplify this activity, provide instruments with very different sounds. To challenge children, provide instruments with similar sounds.

Home Connection

Send home the Family Letter (page 198), suggesting some titles of children's books about music and musicians. Local libraries offer excellent suggestions, such as *What Charlie Heard* (2002) by Mordicai Gerstein and *I See the Rhythm* (2005) by Toyomi Igus. Have children read and discuss the books with their families.

1, 2, 3...Do the Freeze!

Standard

Moves his or her body in a variety of controlled ways

Overview

Children freeze in a position when music stops and attempt to hold their positions.

Materials

- variety of music (e.g., classical, rock and roll, traditional/cultural, and jazz)

Extension

Invite children to dance with a partner, to hold hands or handkerchiefs, or to tie a bandana around their ankles, allowing them to work together to match their dancing to the tempo of the music.

Home Connection

Send home the Family Letter (page 198), suggesting that families play this game using music that adults and children enjoy together. Have children share their experiences from home with the class.

Procedure

1. Invite children to play the Freeze Dance. Explain that they will dance when the music is playing and freeze like statues when the music stops. You may wish to assign a "music controller" if children are working alone in a group.

2. Show children how to move to match the tempo of the music. For example, if the music is upbeat, they may move at a faster pace.

3. Play several rounds of the Freeze Dance. Experiment with different tempos and styles of music, featuring some slow, smooth songs and some faster, upbeat tunes.

Mystery Centers

We are all born with extraordinary powers of imagination, intelligence, feeling, intuition, spirituality, and of physical and sensory awareness. For the most part, we use only a fraction of these powers, and some not at all. Many people have not found their element because they don't understand their own powers.

—Sir Ken Robinson (2009)

Mystery learning centers are not much different from other learning centers in terms of theory and practice; however, they provide children with frequent, visible opportunities to take charge of content and establish their own habits of engagement. For example, teachers may choose to dedicate one center to flexible content. To determine the activities at the Mystery Center, children listen to one another and share their ideas about specific materials or activities. Research supports the idea that creativity is directly related to the amount of open-ended activity children experience. When children experience states of mind in which they are totally engaged—"in the zone" or "wired in"—they are indeed in their element. Another term to describe this is *flow*.

According to Csikszentmihalyi (2008), flow is completely focused motivation. Similar to finding one's "element" (Robinson 2009), flow is a state of mind in which challenging tasks are compatible with the desire and joy involved in the *doing*. "The quality of attention in flow is relaxed yet highly focused. It is a concentration very different from straining to pay attention when we are tired or bored, or when our focus is under siege from intrusive feelings such as anxiety or anger (Goleman 2006, 92). Child-directed, engaging activities maintain joy as the central focus. Mystery Centers provide early childhood teachers and children with endless creative pathways to integrate content in meaningful ways and to promote successful learning.

Superheroes

Standard

Identifies the similarities and differences between persons, places, things, and events using concrete data

Overview

Children identify and share strengths through the lens of superheroes (e.g., what makes someone powerful, different ways to demonstrate power).

Materials

- developmentally appropriate comic books for children to explore
- paper
- colored markers
- crayons

Preparation Note

Select developmentally appropriate comic books to share with children.

Procedure

1. Show children the comics. Notice the features of comics, and ask children to identify what makes these books different from other kinds of books.

2. Discuss the concept of superheroes and what qualities superheroes have that makes them different from other people. Children will likely have specific ideas about powers/abilities, costumes, special names, physical postures/gestures, and helping others.

3. Invite children to draw their own superheroes, using paper, colored markers, and crayons. Suggest that children share their drawings and ideas with peers to answer questions and receive constructive feedback, and to gain inspiration from others' ideas.

4. Ask children to consider people in their community who share some of the qualities they have identified as making someone "super." Some categories might include brain powers, body powers, and caring powers, although these categories are *not* mutually exclusive.

Superheroes *(cont.)*

Extension

Children can create a classroom mural of a cityscape that features their superheroes and where they live. Children will discuss what they know about cities and about the process of designing and executing the mural. In small groups or as a class, children may write letters to people whom they admire, asking questions about the job each person does. This information may contribute to class-made books about various community roles and responsibilities.

Home Connection

Send home the Family Letter (page 198), inviting family members to class to interview for an audio/visual "heroes" library. Children and teachers can design an interview protocol in advance that may be sent home to guests.

Big Store

Standard

Identifies simple problems and possible solutions

Overview

Children create their own Big Store. Children determine what they want to sell, create those items, and "sell" them to their classmates and families.

Materials

- photographs of stores (inside and outside)
- store materials (e.g., empty food containers, boxes, cans, play money, shopping bags, baskets)

Procedure

1. Discuss the idea of a classroom store with children. Examine photographs of familiar stores in the community (including inside the stores, if possible) to articulate design strategies, products for sale, and other qualities.

2. Arrange the center space to embody the Big Store, with consideration given to where items will be stored/shelved and how the flow of foot traffic will move. Also discuss supplies such as money, cash registers, and receipts. Borrow items from dramatic play or other centers as needed.

3. Invite children to discuss what items they would like to sell at their store. They may wish to sell traditional items or create their own unique items. Once children have decided upon a theme for the store, they may create their items, using available materials.

4. Children will designate roles and themes according to their imaginations. Items from dramatic play and other learning centers (e.g., Math, Language and Literacy) can enhance the use of the Big Store.

Big Store *(cont.)*

Extension

Children can create graphs to represent the number of items made and sold. Children can dictate or write letters to neighborhood merchants to ask for advertising tips and to learn about commercial/marketing tools.

 ## Home Connection

Send home the Family Letter (page 198), inviting families to visit the Big Store. Likewise, children from other classrooms may be invited for a special "sale" event.

Food for Thought

Standard

Classifies foods and food combinations according to the food groups

Overview

Children design healthy choices for a classroom restaurant.

Materials

- restaurant materials (e.g., cloth napkins, plates, cups, utensils, plastic food items)
- paper
- crayons
- colored markers
- scissors
- glue
- magazine pictures or advertising circulars with images of food items

Procedure

1. Brainstorm ideas for a restaurant with children, asking them for healthy foods they eat when they go to restaurants. Create a list of ideas so that children can see how much they know about restaurants and healthy food. Have children agree on a theme for the class restaurant, but if there are differing opinions, suggest that the theme will rotate every few days.

2. Invite children to create menus for their restaurant, thinking about healthy foods that will be served. Discuss with children the USDA My Food Plate image, noting the amounts of vegetables, fruits, grains, meat, and dairy that are suggested for people at mealtimes.

3. When children have decided upon foods to serve, they may create menus with paper and art materials. These menus can be laminated for sturdier quality, and children may write on them with dry erase markers.

4. Invite children to decorate the restaurant space, setting up tables and chairs with tablecloths, using items from other centers. Then, open for business!

Food for Thought *(cont.)*

Extension

Explore a specific cultural or ethnic theme with the foods and restaurant decorations. Encourage children to create foods using play dough to supplement the available items.

Home Connection

Send home the Family Letter (page 198), asking families to provide favorite healthy family recipes to create a class cookbook. Once all of the recipes are collected, make copies of the bound pages and send them home for families to enjoy.

Feelings Cards

Standard

Identifies and shares feelings in appropriate ways

Overview

Children learn how to articulate physical and emotional aspects of feelings and to identify the most important or significant parts of a story.

Materials

- cardboard squares or index cards
- colored paper/scrap paper
- glue, scissors
- stickers
- colored markers

Procedure

1. Invite children to tell stories about an important or memorable time. Ask children to remember details about a time when they felt happy, sad, scared, excited, or any other way. Encourage them to think about how they would tell a story about what happened during this important time.

2. Provide the children with several cards to decorate. The cards could represent a sequence of events in their feelings stories or one feeling memory per card.

3. Once children have thought about how they will structure their Feelings Cards, invite older children to use the materials to draw a picture for each card. Younger children may prefer coloring pictures with markers but may use whatever materials best represent their feelings, memories, and visions for their stories.

Feelings Cards *(cont.)*

Extension

Encourage children to create drawings, paintings, collages, or a class book about feelings and emotions. Provide several children's books about feelings in the center, as well as in the Language and Literacy Center.

 ## Home Connection

Send home the Family Letter (page 198), explaining that their children will bring home cards describing a time when they experienced a particular strong emotion. Family members may want to use this opportunity to explore the feelings their child wrote about.

Safety Bingo

Standard

Knows safe behaviors in the classroom and on the playground

Overview

Children play a Bingo game to gain familiarity with simple safety tips and precautions.

Materials

- Safety Picture Cards (page 181)
- Safety Bingo Cards (pages 182–184)
- small objects (will act as Bingo markers)

Preparation Note

Make copies of and cut out the safety picture cards.

Procedure

1. Show children the Safety Picture Cards. Discuss how each picture shows a way to be safe. Discuss why it is important to be safe.

2. Place the Safety Picture Cards facedown in a pile. Explain to children that they will each choose one card and everyone will place an object on the corresponding picture on their Safety Bingo Cards.

3. Distribute Safety Bingo Cards to children. Ask one child to choose one of the Safety Picture Cards. Have all children place an object on the square with the corresponding picture.

Extension

Make these cards available for children to use on their own or in small groups.

Home Connection

Send home the Family Letter (page 198), encouraging children to discuss why safety is so important. You may wish to send home a copy of the Safety Picture Cards and Safety Bingo Cards for families to play at home.

Safety Picture Cards

SPEED LIMIT 35

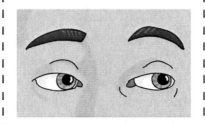

Safety Bingo Cards

Safety Bingo Cards *(cont.)*

Safety Bingo Cards *(cont.)*

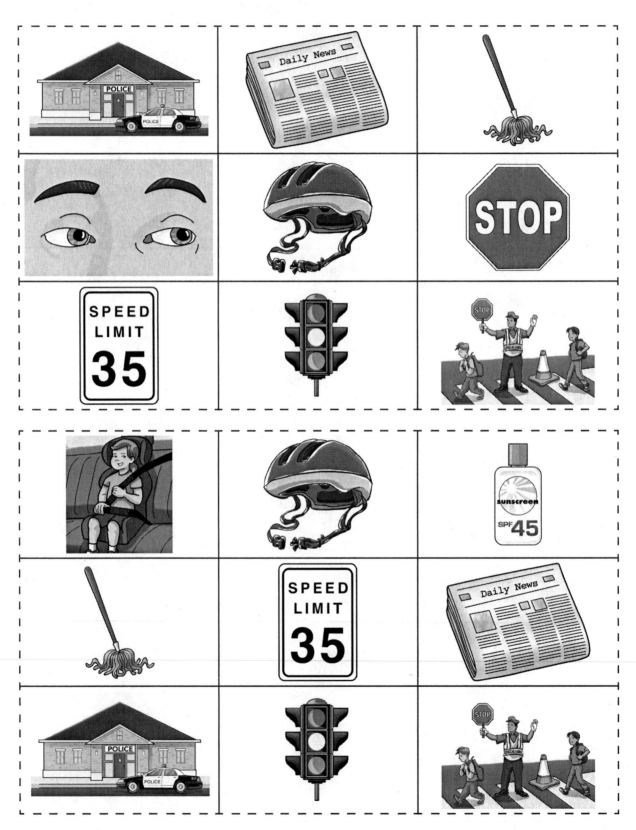

Rainbow Sculptures

Standard

Uses the senses to make observations about living things, nonliving objects, and events

Overview

Children will experiment and observe colored liquids on ice.

Materials

- large brick of ice
- baking dish or pan
- salt (coarse and table)
- food coloring (or liquid watercolors and eyedroppers)

Preparation Note

Prepare a brick of ice by filling an empty half-gallon juice or milk carton with water and freezing it. Remove the carton, and place the ice brick in a shallow glass baking dish or pan large enough to hold two quarts.

Procedure

1. Inform children that they will watch ice turn into a rainbow sculpture that will emerge as they play with the materials. Invite one or two children to pour a liberal amount of salt (coarse salt and/or table salt) over the brick of ice.

2. Ask children to observe what the brick of ice looks like with salt on top of it and to note any changes. Invite them to begin adding drops of food coloring/liquid watercolors to the ice. Encourage them to talk about what they notice happening with the colors.

3. As the salt burrows into the ice, the colors will make visible the tunnels and creases in the brick of ice, shaping the sculpture, and the melting ice will form a colorful puddle in the baking dish.

Rainbow Sculptures (cont.)

Extension

Create smaller blocks of ice for children to use, such as ice cubes and other shapes from molds. Read *The Snowy Day* (1996), by Ezra Jack Keats, and discuss what happens to the snow in that story. Create illustrations about the water cycle, such as rain, ice, and water.

Home Connection

Send home the Family Letter (page 198), encouraging families to make their own Rainbow Sculptures at home, using their own ice shapes of varying sizes. Have families take pictures of their home creations and to share them with the class.

Travel Grab Bags

Standard

Identifies the similarities and differences between persons, places, things, and events using concrete data

Overview

Children explore and become familiar with a specific location and its local culture.

Materials

- large gift bag or sturdy grocery bag decorated with maps and/or a globe

- items representing a specific country and culture (e.g., China: panda bears, chopsticks, Chinese flag; France: beret, postcard of the Eiffel Tower, photos of croissants and other French foods)

Preparation Note

Decorate a Travel Grab Bag that children will place items into.

Procedure

1. Introduce children to the concept of traveling to a different country and learning about different cultures. Explain that you will surprise them by filling the bag with items they can explore in order to learn more about new and exciting people and places.

2. Place a variety of items in the Travel Grab Bags, and invite children to explore the bags in pairs or small groups.

3. Once children have discussed the items and explored each one, ask them to share what they have learned with peers.

Extension

Create Travel Passports for children, providing them with a stamp or a sticker each time they explore and demonstrate knowledge about the different countries and cultures. Encourage older children to create Travel Guides for peers, describing and illustrating what to see, what to eat, what to bring, and other information for people who want to learn more about that country.

 ## Home Connection

Send home the Family Letter (page 198), inviting families to send in items that may be used in Travel Grab Bags, such as postage stamps from different countries, food containers written in different languages, music recordings, and print media.

Some Sort of Garden

Standard

Uses the senses to make observations about living things, nonliving objects, and events

Overview

Children sort seeds into different categories, noticing features and speculating about the kinds of plants they will become. They will plant the seeds, observe the plants growing, and share the plants with members of the community.

Materials

- seeds of different varieties (e.g., zinnias, marigolds, sunflowers, beans, zucchini)
- egg cartons
- soil
- recycled yogurt containers or other containers for potting

Procedure

1. Examine seed packets with children, noting the flowers or plants that the seeds will eventually become. Empty the seeds onto a table, and encourage children to sort the seeds into separate sections of an egg carton.

2. When children have sorted the seeds into different categories (e.g., size, color, texture), they may plant the seeds, using plastic containers as starter pots.

3. As the plants begin to grow, suggest that children observe and record the growth of the leaves, flowers, and buds accordingly during science center time.

4. Identify a local retirement home or senior citizens center for the children to donate their plants. If possible, the class may take a field trip to deliver their plants.

Extension

As the plants grow, they may be transplanted into ceramic pots that the children decorate with paint, glue and tissue paper, or other materials.

 Home Connection

Send home the Family Letter (page 198), suggesting ways children can explore nature and gardening with their families. Suggest children's books about gardening for families to read together, such as *Your First Garden Book* (2009) by Marc Brown, *One Bean* (1999) by Anne Rockwell, and *My Garden* (2010) by Kevin Henkes.

Private Beach

Standard

Knows that Earth materials consist of solid rocks, soils, liquid water, and the gases of the atmosphere

Overview

Children create their own beach jars, which they can use to observe natural elements.

Materials

- small jars with lids
- spoons
- sand
- small shells and sea items
- water
- hot-glue gun (for adult to use)

Procedure

1. Invite children to make their own private beaches. Present the materials to children, and encourage them to explore the sand and sea items.

2. Instruct children to place a few spoonfuls of sand into their jars, until there is approximately one inch of sand in each child's jar.

3. Ask children to select a few items to place in their jars, such as shells, miniature sand dollars, or sea stars.

4. Add water to the jars until the jars are almost full, leaving about $\frac{1}{2}"$ of space at the top.

5. Use a hot-glue gun (teachers only) to spread glue around the inside of the lids and screw the lids onto the jars. Allow the glue time to dry.

Extension

With leftover materials, invite children to make beach collages or beach greeting cards.

Home Connection

Send home the Family Letter (page 198), inviting families to share photos of beach visits or water play with the class. Children can write about their memories and favorite beaches.

Gratitude Letters

Standard

Knows that writing, including pictures, letters, and words, communicates meaning and information

Overview

Children write letters to others, expressing gratitude to help cultivate a positive mindset, self-confidence, and community well-being.

Materials

- paper and envelopes
- pencils
- crayons and colored markers
- postage stamps

Procedure

1. Discuss the word *gratitude* with children. Have them think about what they have to be grateful for. Provide examples such as being grateful for someone who helps clean the classroom or when a child waves hello.

2. Explain to children that they will each write a letter to one person in the class to let him or her know what what the sender is grateful for. Distribute paper and pencils to children. Encourage them to write or draw a letter to a friend, noting two or three things for which they are grateful, and sealing it in an envelope. You may wish to review the letters prior to sealing the envelopes. Be sure to have children write the name of the person on the outside of the envelope. You may wish to assign children a person to write the letter to so that there are no hurt feelings about not receiving a letter.

3. Assist children with their letters as needed.

4. As a class, mail or pass out all of the letters together. Ask children to let you know when they receive their letters at home and what they thought when they read the letter.

Gratitude Letters *(cont.)*

Extension

Children can read books about the art of writing letters and printing and can write additional letters of gratitude.

Home Connection

Send home the Family Letter (page 198), asking children to discuss with their families people who do things for them. For example, a grandma may help babysit or the mailman brings them the mail each day. You may also wish to suggest families read *Frog and Toad: The Letter* (2003) by Arnold Lobel.

References Cited

Biller, Lowell. *Creating Brain-Friendly Classrooms: Practical Instructional Strategies for Educators.* Lanham, MD: Scarecrow Press, Inc, 2003.

Cappiello, Mary Ann, and Erika Thulin Dawes. *Teaching with Text Sets.* Huntington Beach, CA: Shell Education, 2012.

Carlsson-Paige, Nancy. "My view: Obama, Romney Need to Know One Thing About Early Childhood Education—Start Over." 2012. http://schoolsofthought.blogs.cnn.com/2012/08/29/

Carlsson-Paige, Nancy. *Taking Back Childhood: A Proven Road Map for Raising Confident, Creative, Compassionate Kids.* New York: Plume, 2009.

Cooper, Patricia M. *The Classrooms all Young Children Need: Lessons in Teaching from Vivian Paley.* Chicago: The University of Chicago Press, 2011.

Csikszentmihalyi, Mihaly. *Flow: The Psychology of Optimal Experience.* New York: HarperCollins Publishers, 2008.

Diller, Debbie. *Math Work Stations: Independent Learning You Can Count on, K–2.* Portland, ME: Stenhouse Publishers, 2011.

Early Childhood Advisory Council to the Massachusetts Board of Education. *Guidelines for Preschool Learning Experiences."* Malden, MA: Massachusetts Department of Education, 2003.

Edwards, Caroline, Lella Gandini, and George Forman. *The Hundred Languages of Children: The Reggio Emilia Experience in Transformation.* Santa Barbara, CA: Praeger, 2011.

Fiore, Lisa B. *Assessment of Young Children: A Collaborative Approach.* New York: Routledge, 2012.

Fiore, Lisa B. *LifeSmart: Exploring Human Development.* New York: McGraw-Hill, 2011.

Fiore, Lisa B., and Barbara Rosenquest. "Shifting the Culture of Higher Education: Influences on Students, Teachers, and Pedagogy." *Theory Into Practice* (49)1 (2010):14–20.

Fountas, Irene C., and Gay S. Pinnell. *Guided Reading: Good First Teaching for All Children.* Portsmouth, NH: Heinemann, 1996.

Frost, Joe L. *A History of Children's Play and Play Environments: Toward a Contemporary Child-Saving Movement.* New York: Routledge, 2010.

Gewertz, Catherine. "Educators in Search of Common-Core Resources." *Education Week,* 31(22) (2012): 12–13.

Goleman, Daniel. *Emotional Intelligence: Why It Can Matter More Than IQ.* New York: Bantam, 2006.

References Cited *(cont.)*

Hattie, John. *Visible Learning for Teachers: Maximizing Impact on Learning.* New York: Routledge, 2012.

Henig, Robin M. "Taking Play Seriously." 2008. http://www.nytimes.com/2008/02/17/magazine/17play.html.

Hughes, Bob. *Evolutionary Playwork, (2nd Edition).* New York: Routledge, 2012.

Kantrowitz, Barbara, and Pat Wingert. 1991. "The 10 Best Schools in the World." *Newsweek,* 1991, 50–59.

Meier, Deborah, Brenda S. Engel, and Beth Taylor. *Playing for Keeps: Life and Learning on a Public School Playground.* New York: Teachers College Press, 2010.

New, Rebecca S. "Reggio Emilia as Cultural Activity Theory in Practice." *Theory Into Practice* 46(1) (2007): 5–13.

Paley, Vivian. "On Listening to What the Children Say." *Harvard Educational Review* 56(20) (1986): 122–131.

Prince, Michael. "Does Active Learning Work? A Review of the Research." *Journal of Engineering Education* 93(3) (2004): 223–231.

Rinaldi, Carlina. 2001. "Documentation and Assessment: What is the Relationship? In *Making Learning Visible: Children as Individual and Group Learners." Reggio Emilia, Italy: Reggio Children srl* (2001): 78–79.

Rinaldi, Carlina. *In Dialogue with Reggio Emilia: Listening, Researching, and Learning.* New York: Routledge, 2006.

Robinson, Ken, and Lou Aronica. *The Element: How Finding Your Passion Changes Everything.* New York: Penguin Books, 2009.

Turner, Terri, and Daniel G. Wilson. "Reflections on Documentation: A Discussion With Thought Leaders from Reggio Emilia." *Theory Into Practice* 49(1) (2010): 5–13.

Recommended Resources

Recommended Books

Brown, M. 1981. *Your First Garden Book*. Little Brown and Co.

Gerstein, M. 2002. *What Charlie Heard*. Farrar, Straus, and Giroux.

Henkes, K. 2010. *My Garden*. Greenwillow Books.

Igus, T.I. 2005. *I See the Rhythm*. Lee and Low Book, Inc.

Juster, N. 2000. *The Dot and the Line*. Chronicle Books.

Keats, E.J. 1996. *The Snowy Day*. Viking Juvenile.

Lionni, L. 1995. *Little Blue and Little Yellow*. HarperCollins.

Lobel, A. 2003. *Frog and Toad: The Letter*. HarperCollins.

Paley, V. 1998. *The Girl with the Brown Crayon: How Children Use Stories to Shape Their Lives*. Harvard University Press.

Pinto, S. 2003. *The Alphabet Room*. Bloomsbury USA Children's Books.

Rockwell, A. 1999. *One Bean*. Walker Childrens.

Shaw, C.G. 1993. *It Looked Like Spilt Milk*. HarperFestival.

Wiesner, D. 2006. *Flotsam*. Clarion Books.

Recommended Websites

Technology

Free Technology for Teachers: http://www.freetech4teachers.com/

> This site features a blog written by educator Richard Byrne. The various links provide teachers of various age/grade levels with an endless source of lesson plans, activities, and inspiration for ways to incorporate technology into their work with students.

TeacherTube: http://www1.teachertube.com/

> For those accustomed to YouTube, TeacherTube will feel quite familiar. This website features videos created by teachers so that they may share their ideas and receive feedback from a global online community. Teachers post videos and lessons, and there are groups for educators to join by topics of interest.

Recommended Resources *(cont.)*

Research on Early Childhood Learning

The Wonder of Learning: http://www.thewonderoflearning.com/

This website provides stunning visual examples of documentation from early childhood infant-toddler centers and preschools in Reggio Emilia, Italy. The individual sections celebrate children as active, curious, and competent learners. The traveling exhibition has been widely appealing to early childhood educators in the United States and around the world, and inspiration can be gained by exploring the various site offerings.

Council of Chief State School Officers (CCSSO): http://www.ccsso.org/resources/programs/interstate_teacher_assessment_consortium_(intasc).html

This website provides access to resources related to the INTASC standards. Publications, programs, and resources inform educators about accountability and what all teachers should know and be able to do. Specific material relating to early childhood is available using a simple search bar.

Math Centers

Math Pickle: http://www.mathpickle.com/K-12/Videos_K-2.html

This site features videos for K–2 educators, illustrating math lessons and resources in engaging videos featuring familiar resources. The home site includes videos for K–12 students, so early childhood teachers may also find inspiration in activities designed for older children.

Copy/Paste: http://www.peterpappas.com/2011/06/dont-teach-them-facts-let-student-discover-patterns.html

This entry is one of several useful and provocative entries in the Copy/Paste blog. In this entry, Mr. Pappas shares some thoughts about the importance of patterns, and suggested interesting entries are provided. The site features links to videos and other educator-authored blogs.

Literacy Centers

The Classroom Bookshelf: http://classroombookshelf.blogspot.com/

This blog is co-authored and maintained by educators Mary Ann Cappiello, Erika Thulin Dawes, and Grace Enriquez. Each week, they introduce a recently published book with three areas of focus—Book Review, Teaching Invitations, and Further Explorations. Archives to previous postings make a wealth of information available in an incredible range of topics.

The International Reading Association: http://www.reading.org/

This professional organization proudly engages over 60,000 members in worldwide literacy efforts. Dedicated to a host of activities, the site features resources designed specifically for teachers and parents as well as timely information relating to standards and accountability. This site provides excellent access to a global network of professionals in a variety of settings.

Recommended Resources (cont.)

Science Centers

The San Francisco Exploratorium: http://www.exploratorium.edu/

This site provides a tremendous amount of information, resources, and interactive activity relating to science, art, and human perception. There are sections dedicated to broad categories as well as invitations for people to explore based on who they are—teen, parent, educator, and so on.

Boston Museum of Science: http://www.mos.org/educators

This website is designed for educators to use and enjoy as they learn about science and make it meaningful for students of various ages. Resources are provided for classroom use as well as for proposed field trips. Professional development opportunities and links to exhibitions are featured.

Social Studies

Smithsonian Kids: http://www.si.edu/Kids

This site provides access to websites for all of the Smithsonian museums, highlighting opportunities for children, families, and educators. Guides to current and permanent exhibitions and collections are included. Online activities engage children from the comfort of their own classrooms and/or homes.

UNICEF Child-Friendly Cities: http://www.childfriendlycities.org

This website provides visitors with important information about UNICEF's commitment to building child-friendly communities. These efforts grew out of the Convention on the Rights of the Child, supported by members of the United Nations. Case examples, recent research, and criteria for action plans illustrate citizens' efforts and initiatives.

Art Centers

The Eric Carle Museum of Picture Book Art: http://www.carlemuseum.org/

This website is visually stunning, and provides a wealth of information for children, parents, teachers, and the general public. There are resources available such as lesson plans, activities, and book lists as well as information about exhibitions and professional development opportunities.

smART kids: http://smartmuseum.uchicago.edu/smartkids

This engaging, interactive site is connected to the David and Alfred Smart Museum of Art at the University of Chicago. The site features material for parents and educators, and teaches children about art while they experience it for themselves. Children learn about art vocabulary and act as art detectives. The Sketch Book feature is something that children will ask to visit and revisit.

Recommended Resources (cont.)

Music Centers

National Jukebox: http://www.loc.gov/jukebox/

This website features historical sound recordings from the Library of Congress. Over 100 years of music, technology, and innovation are available at no cost, organized by artists, genres, and playlists among other categories.

Imagine: http://imagine.musictherapy.biz/Imagine/home.html

This site presents archives and current issues of *Imagine*, the early childhood online magazine of the American Music Therapy Association. The magazine provides easy access to research and educational materials supporting the benefits of music in early childhood.

World Cultural Dance: http://www.fitforafeast.com/dance_cultural.htm

Discover various folk dances from around the world.

Mystery Centers

Mindfulness in Education Network: http://www.mindfuled.org/

The Mindfulness in Education Network supports a growing number of professionals committed to enhancing the potential of all children in educational settings through contemplative practices. The organization strives to inspire collaboration in its efforts to bring a focus to joy in learning.

StoryCorps: http://storycorps.org/

The StoryCorps website emphasizes the importance of stories in human development and human connections and the tremendous power of listening. There are resources for educators, opportunities to get involved in your local community, and engaging animated pieces that young children and adults can enjoy.

Family Letter

Dear Families,

   We have been working on _____
this week during center time in class.

   You are critical to the success of our learning centers and the children's success as learners! It would be very helpful to your child if you could:

_____

_____

_____

_____

_____

_____

   I look forward to learning with your children, and to answering any questions you may have.

Sincerely,

_____

How Learning Centers Support English Language Learners

To support learning experiences for children in their native languages, consider the following strategies:

- Encourage children to demonstrate what they know through drawing, writing, using physical models or representations, and other concrete, nonverbal means.

- Encourage children to speak and experiment with language.

- Encourage social interactions and collaboration.

- Include books, art, music, and dramatic play materials that represent many cultures and feature many languages.

- Ensure that the native languages of *all* children in the group are visible *and* readily available to be heard.

To promote success at learning centers, consider the following strategies:

- Start by using many words that are already familiar to children, such as their own names and classroom materials.

- Repeat instructions for activities often, modeling use of materials and behavior.

- Provide children with feedback daily throughout every learning center period, such as describing and summarizing what they worked on, played with, completed, and learned.

- Share your observations with them, using vocabulary specific to the activities to help them form associations among words, actions, and materials.

- Validate children's efforts by responding to their questions and attempts at problem solving.

- Provide children with adult support and encourage peer support.

- Maintain a positive attitude toward risk taking and creative expression.

A Guide for the First 6 Weeks— Getting Started with Centers

Weeks 1 and 2	
Ideas for Working with Children	**Ideas for Materials**
• Engage children in large-group activities. • Design activities that encourage collaboration and social interaction; Activities should include short-term projects that they can finish and take home to share with families. • Walk children through the many areas in the room and generate ideas about how to work in them. • Play and work in the different areas of the room • Provide children with clear directions, model behavior with them, and observe students' progress. • Introduce children's names (and icons, if using icons); place these in multiple areas around the room. • Praise children for their effort as well as for their responsible use of classroom materials.	• Designate and maintain a spacious area for large-group work. • Choose simple materials that are well organized. • Place children's names and pictures up in every part of the room (e.g., name chart, helper chart, stories about them, name cards).

Weeks 3 and 4	
Ideas for Working with Children	**Ideas for Materials**
• Open new areas one at a time, providing explicit instruction for use of and storage of materials. • Begin to have children play in small groups in the centers. Observe the process and praise their effort and self-regulation. • Begin to play and work with individuals while other children are working independently in centers.	• Each time a new center opens, have materials organized in a standard way, with materials labeled and accessible and visible storage areas for all materials. • Identify a consistent and visible table location for yourself so that you can observe the whole class even while working with individuals or small groups of children.

A Guide for the First 6 Weeks—
Getting Started with Centers *(cont.)*

Weeks 5 and 6	
Ideas for Working with Children	**Ideas for Materials**
• Establish routines for working in small groups in centers for a period of time, building up to one hour. • Emphasize the importance of individual and group work accordingly. • Introduce tools for managing learning center activity (e.g., chart, craft sticks) and help children use them. • Begin with 2–3 activities, and visit children throughout the classroom to better gauge children's understanding of the routines. • Identify times for individual and small-group assessment. • Introduce children to self-assessment tools.	• Introduce new materials gradually. • Display products of individual and group work. • Establish places for work in progress to be kept and revisited.

Adapted from Fountas & Pinnell (1996)

Planning Tool—Learning Centers

Name: _____

Directions: Mark an *X* on the days you will complete each content-area center.

	Monday	Tuesday	Wednesday	Thursday	Friday
Math					
Language and Literacy					
Science					
Social Studies					
Art					
Music					
Mystery					

Planning Tool—Activities

Name: _____

Directions: Put a sticker on each circle when you finish your work at each learning center.

Math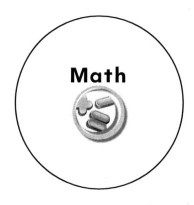

Science

Music

Language and Literacy

Mystery

Social Studies

Art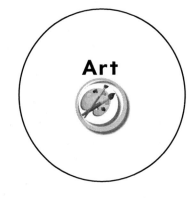

Reflection: Does Classroom Design Support Learning Center Use and Value?

☐ 1. Are there well-defined areas for large-group, small-group, and individual activities?

☐ 2. Are there areas for children to enjoy quiet, independent work?

☐ 3. Are centers arranged so that the teacher(s) can observe the whole classroom?

☐ 4. Are center management tools (e.g., chart, board) strategically located and in clear view?

☐ 5. Are written directions that feature images as well as text available at every center?

☐ 6. Are classroom materials inviting, well organized, and accessible for all children?

☐ 7. Are there distinct, safe places to store children's completed work and work in progress?